Sometimes it takes someone from a foreign [...] impact of the USA on its version of evangelicalism. Add to that a person's excruciating experiences among evangelicals. Both can provoke serious questions about the integrity and faithfulness of the movement. Con Campbell has watched American evangelicalism from afar and up close, and he has experienced one of life's biggest tragedies. This book is a testimony of his experience within evangelicalism as one of its leaders, in the USA and abroad, and it becomes through his pain a heartfelt plea that evangelicalism turn back to Jesus to rediscover all over again the way of Jesus. *Jesus v. Evangelicals* is a painful healing many of us need.

—**SCOT MCKNIGHT**, author, *A Church Called Tov*; pastor; professor of New Testament, Northern Seminary

What happens in America never stays in America. We are only kidding ourselves to think that our Christian brothers and sisters are unaware of or untouched by the hostile divisions, politicization, abuse scandals, and tribalism infecting American evangelicalism. The whole world witnessed the violence at the US Capitol on January 6 with rioters waving Jesus banners. For Australian biblical scholar Constantine Campbell, this crisis is alarming, destructive, and profoundly personal. He has the wounds to prove it. This is not the Christianity of Jesus. *Jesus v. Evangelicals* is Campbell's foray into understanding and uprooting underlying causes of this crisis and to find ways, as they say, to right the ship. This book points readers back to Jesus.

—**CAROLYN CUSTIS JAMES**, author, *Half the Church* and *Malestrom*

Con Campbell knows the American evangelical scene from the inside, yet he offers an outsider's perspective of a movement that he believes has gone astray. Using a mixture of cultural commentary and biblical insights, Campbell puts his finger on the lies and lunacies that get trotted out in the name of Christ in American circles. This is not an elitist critique of popular American religion, it is calling America back to the religion of Jesus and the apostles.

—**DR. MICHAEL F. BIRD**, author, *Religious Freedom in the Secular Age*; academic dean and lecturer in New Testament, Ridley College, Melbourne, Australia

With *Jesus v. Evangelicals*, Constantine Campbell does not wade into the shallow end of the pool of controversial topics that Christians fight about but dives fully into the deep! This book will surely annoy some people, but it will motivate others because Campbell's thoughtful, biblical, vulnerable, and culturally astute analysis can help chart a new and better course. I applaud him for bringing his scholarship and personal experience to challenge the status quo.

—**DENNIS R. EDWARDS**, dean, North Park Theological Seminary

Campbell holds up a light as much as a mirror in this breathtakingly important book, asking fellow Christians to take responsibility for their commitments to themselves and others by offering close readings of Scripture in conversation with contemporary evangelical life. Taking account of institutions and attitudes that create division and confusion, Campbell offers intellectual clarity and spiritual charity in equal measure as he walks the reader through his own relationship with the biblical text and the Christian worlds he inhabits, observing rifts between evangelicals and their larger communities. But just as important, he shares thoughts on how those rifts can be mended in an enduring, meaningful, and honest way. This book matters not only to evangelicals but also to those outside of the evangelical community who care about what happens to their neighbors who live within it and want to better understand the struggles they face.

—**MARK LEUCHTER**, professor, Hebrew Bible and ancient Judaism, Temple University, Philadelphia

JESUS

v.

EVANGELICALS

JESUS

v.

EVANGELICALS

*A **Biblical Critique** of a Wayward Movement*

CONSTANTINE R. CAMPBELL

ZONDERVAN
REFLECTIVE

ZONDERVAN REFLECTIVE

Jesus v. Evangelicals
Copyright © 2023 by Constantine R. Campbell

Requests for information should be addressed to:
Zondervan, *3900 Sparks Dr. SE, Grand Rapids, Michigan 49546*

Zondervan titles may be purchased in bulk for educational, business, fundraising, or sales promotional use. For information, please email SpecialMarkets@Zondervan.com.

ISBN 978-0-310-13544-9 (softcover)
ISBN 978-0-310-13576-0 (audio)
ISBN 978-0-310-13545-6 (ebook)

Cover design: Darren Welch
Cover images: © Viniclus Tupinamba; Donatas1205 / Shutterstock
Interior design: Sara Colley

Printed in the United States of America

22 23 24 25 26 27 28 29 30   /TRM/   12 11 10 9 8 7 6 5 4 3 2 1

For Niah

CONTENTS

ACKNOWLEDGMENTS

THIS WAS A RISKY BOOK TO WRITE. WHILE I HAVE ALWAYS depended on others' feedback and encouragement as I've worked on previous books, I needed more of both for this one. Once again I offer my thanks to the team at Zondervan, especially to Stan Gundry, Ryan Pazdur, Brian Phipps, Alexis De Weese, and the one and only Katya Covrett. It's a risky book for them too and I admire their chutzpah.

A number of friends helped with the manuscript, which is significantly stronger for their input. In particular, I owe a debt of thanks to Graham Cole, Andrew Judd, George Athas, Joseph Luigs, David Croteau, Maria Custodio, Dan Anderson, and Phillip Palacios.

Finally, I want to thank my gorgeous wife, Niah, to whom this book is dedicated. Not only did she read the manuscript multiple times through its various iterations, offering excellent feedback, but she regularly discussed many of the ideas, issues, and difficulties with me as I wrote—virtually every day that I wrote. Her consistent and sincere encouragement propelled me, and her practical partnership facilitated the entire project. I would not have been able to write this book without her. Thanks, babe. You are a gift from God.

INTRODUCTION

"CAN YOU BELIEVE PEOPLE BELIEVE THAT BULLSHIT?"

So said Donald Trump after a meeting in 2012 with pastors who laid hands on him in prayer, according to Michael Cohen, Trump's former lawyer and confidant.[1] That may be the most honest thing Trump ever said about evangelicals, and in one sentence he perfectly captured the zeitgeist. Ironically, evangelical support of Donald Trump is one of the main reasons why critics today regard evangelicalism as, well, BS.

Commentator Peter Wehner writes, "It's hard to imagine a person who has less affinity for authentic Christianity—for the teachings of Jesus, from the Sermon on the Mount to the parable of the Good Samaritan—than Donald Trump." And by overlooking and excusing Trump's corrupt character and actions, evangelicals "have forfeited the right to ever again argue that character counts in America's political leaders."[2] It is hardly surprising, then, to witness "increasing disaffection among white millennial and Gen X evangelicals with the cultural and political preoccupations that have strongly motivated their parents and grandparents," as religion scholar Terry Shoemaker's research reveals.[3] And the fallout goes well beyond the political realm, with as many as 25 million disenfranchised evangelicals fleeing the movement in recent years.[4]

The focus of this book is American evangelicalism, but it is not limited to it. The issues raised here are relevant to all evangelicals wherever they live. The sheer dominance of the US globally has far-reaching consequences for all evangelicals, whether Australian, British, Kenyan, or whatever. American evangelicalism is massively influential beyond US borders. But American evangelicalism is at a crisis point, a movement in disarray. Evangelicals are faced with a quandary: Will they double down and continue along this perilous path of compromise with political parties, or will they stop, reflect, and change course? And while support of Donald Trump has produced the tipping point of the evangelical crisis, it is not by any means evangelicalism's only problem.

WHO IS AN EVANGELICAL?

Before we may critique evangelicalism, we must know what we are critiquing. One of the challenges we face is understanding what on earth the term actually means. Who is an evangelical?[5] The answer depends on who you ask.

The starting point is to recognize that evangelicalism is a big tent. It is not a monolithic movement that can easily be defined. And it is difficult to survey this big tent without some appreciation of the history of the movement. While I will occasionally touch on this history, I'm not a historian, so I rely on experts such as George Marsden, David Bebbington, Mark Noll, John Fea, Thomas Kidd, and Kristin Kobes Du Mez, among others.

The classic definition of historic British evangelicalism comes from Bebbington, whose "quadrilateral" is mostly theological. "There are the four qualities that have been the special mark of Evangelical religion: *conversionism*, the belief that lives need to be changed; *activism*, the expression of the gospel in effort; *biblicism*, a particular regard for the Bible; and what may be called *crucicentrism*, a stress on the sacrifice of Christ on the cross. Together they form a quadrilateral of priorities that is the basis of Evangelicalism."[6]

Marsden's description of eighteenth- and nineteenth-century evangelicalism bridges the Atlantic with a common theological focus on the death of Christ. "'Evangelical' (from the Greek word for 'gospel') eventually became the common British and American name for the revival movements that swept back and forth across the English-speaking world and elsewhere during the eighteenth and nineteenth centuries. Central to the evangelical gospel was the proclamation of Christ's saving work through his death on the cross and the necessity of personally trusting him for eternal salvation."[7]

This laid the groundwork for contemporary evangelicalism, as Marsden extrapolates. "Roughly speaking, evangelicalism today includes any Christians traditional enough to affirm the basic beliefs of the old nineteenth-century evangelical consensus. The essential evangelical beliefs include (1) the Reformation doctrine of the final authority of the Bible, (2) the real historical character of God's saving work recorded in Scripture, (3) salvation to eternal life based on the redemptive work of Christ, (4) the importance of evangelism and missions, and (5) the importance of a spiritually transformed life."[8]

But today it could be argued that evangelicalism's cultural

influence has overshadowed its theological heritage, as suggested by American political scientist and sociologist Alan Wolfe. According to Wolfe, American religions have begun to resemble each other in their cultural practice, and most of all that of evangelicals, so that there is "a sense in which we are all Evangelicals now."[9] These similarities include the rhetoric of praise and worship songs, sermons, and writing. Casual dress, contemporary music, and enthusiastic atmospheres differentiate evangelical culture from mainline traditional forms of worship. There is also a turn of focus away from God and toward the self in seeking comfort, intimacy, and answers to felt needs in worship.[10] And in the public sphere, evangelicalism's political nature has begun to overshadow its theological heritage. According to Du Mez, "Despite evangelicals' frequent claims that the Bible is the source of their social and political commitments, evangelicalism must be seen as a cultural and political movement rather than as a community defined chiefly by its theology."[11]

Some might prefer to subdivide evangelicalism according to location, acknowledging the differences between American evangelicals, British evangelicals, Korean evangelicals, Australian evangelicals, and so forth. So historian Mark Noll writes, "The rapid expansion of evangelical-like movements around the world presents a . . . challenge to any coherent understanding of evangelicalism."[12] While that subdivision makes sense, it is not sufficient anymore given the cross-pollination that now occurs through modern media and communication. A better subdivision is to think of evangelicalism as having three major strands—theological evangelicals, cultural evangelicals, and political evangelicals. Often these categories overlap significantly. While some evangelicals may belong to only one of these categories, I contend that if someone does not belong to any of the three, they are not in any meaningful sense an evangelical.

Theological evangelicals are those Christians who are evangelical by conviction. They regard the Bible as God's authoritative Word, which teaches that Jesus is the Son of God, who died for the sins of humanity to reconcile us to God and to grant eternal life. This kind of evangelical has the best historical claim to the term, since these theological convictions have been part of evangelicalism since the Protestant Reformation in the sixteenth century.

Cultural evangelicals are those Christians who have adopted a way of life, community, and worship that has been informed by theological evangelicalism. They are not necessarily evangelical by conviction but identify as evangelical because of the crowd they run in.

Political evangelicals are not necessarily evangelical by theological conviction or culture, but they share a set of political commitments that have come to be known as evangelical. Anyone who calls themselves an evangelical today or is called one by others will fit in at least one of these groups. Many will fit two or all three.

The blurriness between these three groups partly accounts for the confusion around the term *evangelical*. Church leaders tend to use it to refer to the first group—theological evangelicals. Social commentators and general media tend to use it for the second group—cultural evangelicals. And political commentators and news media tend to use the term for the third group—political evangelicals. This blurriness also makes it difficult to critique evangelicalism. If a criticism is leveled against political evangelicals, for example, theological evangelicals might simply deny the charge, and vice versa. To make matters more complicated, further subdivisions are possible. Theological evangelicals can be Calvinist or Arminian, egalitarian or complementarian, inerrantist or infallibilist. Cultural evangelicals can be suburban warriors, city bohos, or country bumpkins. Political evangelicals are mostly right-wing Republicans, but there are some left-leaning political evangelicals too. We won't get into the weeds with these subdivisions. This is simply a recognition of the "sheer, mind-boggling diversity" within the world of evangelicalism that Noll describes.[13] Given such complexity, some evangelicals will agree with almost everything in this book; others almost nothing. Some will be offended by my critique; others will rejoice. Some evangelicals will want to course correct; others will double down. *C'est la vie.*

However legitimate these subdivisions are, Marsden concludes that they are connected to each other in a single movement. "Evangelicalism, then, despite its diversities, is properly spoken of as a single movement in at least two different ways. It is a broader movement somewhat unified by common heritages, influences, problems, and tendencies. It is also a conscious fellowship, coalition, community family, or feudal system of friends and rivals who have some stronger sense of belonging together. These 'evangelicals' constitute something like a denomination, although a most informal one."[14]

For better or worse, all three evangelical subgroups (theological, cultural, political) are in some sense tied to each other as they continue to identify with the movement bearing the name evangelical. Since no one owns language, theological evangelicals cannot claim that political evangelicals are not really evangelicals. If political evangelicals identify themselves as such—or if others do—there is a sense in which they too are evangelicals whether or not other evangelicals like it. This, then, is my disclaimer for using the term *evangelical* in a very broad way. I recognize that there are various types of evangelicals and that one description does not do justice to all, but at the same time, there is such a thing as evangelicalism as a whole—as messy, ill defined, and sometimes self-contradictory as it is.

WHO AM I?

I'm an evangelical. Or at least I used to be. I don't know anymore. In that sense, I relate to a growing number of evangelicals—or former evangelicals—who are likewise experiencing a crisis of identity. I have an evangelical heritage. I became a Christian in an independent evangelical church while studying music at the Australian National University, in Canberra, Australia. I later trained at the evangelical Anglican seminary in Sydney—Moore College—where I ended up lecturing in New Testament after serving as a pastor in my home church. I was ordained as a deacon in the evangelical Anglican diocese of Sydney. Then I was professor of New Testament at Trinity Evangelical Divinity School in Illinois. While living in the Chicago area, I attended an Evangelical Free Church, where I regularly preached. Many of my publications have been released by evangelical publishing houses, such as Zondervan, Baker, and Eerdmans, and I have presented papers at the Evangelical Theological Society.

But for years I have been a quiet critic of evangelicalism. Many of the ideas in this book were workshopped in classrooms as my students and I wrestled with the text of the Bible and evangelical faith and culture. My central evangelical conviction is to allow the Bible to shape all other convictions. I have therefore resisted checking boxes for the sake of evangelical orthodoxy whenever I viewed the Scriptures leading in a different direction. If the Bible offers a critique of evangelical faith and practice, then so be it. And if the title and subtitle of this book didn't tip you off, I believe the Bible does offer such a critique.

My increasing disillusionment with the movement we call evangelicalism has not weakened my respect for Jesus or the Bible. While I might be ready to jettison *evangelicalism*—depending on what that means—I'm not planning to jettison Jesus or the Bible. On the contrary, the approach of this book is to measure evangelicalism against them. The moment any Christian faith ceases to be critiqued and shaped by Jesus is the moment it is no longer a biblical faith. As self-proclaimed Bible people, evangelicals ought to be prepared to do the hard work of biblical self-examination. Above all else, a healthy and robust evangelicalism is committed to truth, regardless of how uncomfortable that may be. As I often said to my students, we have nothing to fear from the truth. We ought to be glad if we find ourselves corrected by it.

WHAT'S WRONG WITH EVANGELICALISM?

What's wrong with evangelicalism? Some critics may answer, "Everything!" But that is hardly fair. Evangelicalism has a distinguished heritage that can lay claim to the compositions of J. S. Bach, the theology and philosophy of Jonathan Edwards, the hymnody of Charles Wesley, the preaching of George

Whitefield, William Wilberforce's abolition of the British slave trade, Harriet Beecher Stowe's antislavery novel *Uncle Tom's Cabin*, Harriet Tubman's underground emancipation of slaves, Florence Nightingale's revolution of modern nursing, Bob Pierce's founding of World Vision International, Billy Graham's global ecumenism, John Stott's biblical expositions, Joni Eareckson Tada's disability advocacy, and the visual artwork of Makoto Fujimura—to name just a few of evangelicalism's treasures. But above all, the central feature of historic evangelicalism is its advocacy of vibrant personal faith in Jesus. It's not the pursuit of Jesus that's failing contemporary evangelicalism but the failure to pursue Jesus in favor of other pursuits. *New York Times* columnist Ross Douthat proposes that "America's problem isn't too much religion, or too little of it. It's *bad* religion: the slow-motion collapse of traditional Christianity and the rise of a variety of destructive pseudo-Christianities in its place."[15] The path of evangelicalism during the second half of the twentieth century till now has contributed to this "slow-motion collapse." And it could be claimed that it is becoming or has become one of those pseudo-Christianities.

THE SYMPTOMS OF ILLNESS

The first problem to address is epistemological: How do evangelicals know what they know? Evangelicals regard themselves as "the Bible people," which means they seek to treat the Scriptures as the highest authority in matters of life and faith. But this commitment to the Bible can unwittingly block critique. If, for example, a nonevangelical claims that evangelicals are wrong about this or that, it is relatively easy to dismiss their critique by saying that to disagree with them is to disagree with the Bible. But such thinking creates a totalitarian approach to truth, placing beliefs beyond honest criticism. The most dangerous people are those who believe they speak the truth but do not. The obvious question is, How do you know whether you are speaking the truth? The first step toward epistemic confidence must be epistemic humility. If we are not first willing to question how we know what we know, and to consider challenges to the veracity of our truth claims, we will be doomed to our modes of thought with all of their mistakes, narrowness, and prejudices. So I humbly ask anyone reading this to take a deep breath and consider whether there's some truth to the critiques to come.

The scope of this book is wide ranging, but it does not offer a comprehensive critique of evangelicalism. While critics may identify other issues left unaddressed, the book offers the following criticisms.

- American evangelicalism in particular has become politicized to the extent that its spiritual nature has been distorted.
- Evangelicals tend to have an "us versus them" mentality toward outsiders.
- Evangelicalism suffers from the perception and reality of judgmentalism.
- Evangelicals are often highly divisive, exacerbating theological and cultural divisions that create tribal boundaries.
- Evangelicals have an understood code of acceptable and unacceptable sins.

- Evangelicals tend to shoot their wounded by the way they treat marriage failure, divorce, and remarriage.
- Many evangelicals celebrate potentially unhealthy church models.
- The popular face of evangelicalism has been overrun by those peddling false gospels.
- The term *evangelical* no longer means what it once did, posing a significant problem for all evangelicals.

As serious as they are, I contend that these problems are merely symptoms of a deeper illness. If that's right, what is the illness? And what is its remedy?

ONE

GOD AND COUNTRY

My kingdom is not of this world.

MANY AMERICANS BELIEVE THAT AMERICA IS GOD'S COUNTRY. Some also think that this belief obligates them to fight for the preservation of Christian culture and political influence. In 2010, the Public Religion Research Institute found that while 60 percent of Americans believed that God has granted America a special role in human history, the same view was held by 80 percent of white evangelicals.[1] This notion finds its roots in the European settlement of North America, when the majority of early Pilgrims were Puritans pursuing greater religious freedom. They wanted to "finish the [Protestant] Reformation" without fear of recrimination and believed they had found their opportunity in the new world.[2] Free from institutionalized religion and prescribed worship, the Pilgrims understood their new home as God's abundant blessing. It was the new Israel—the promised land—where God would be honored by true worshipers who were free to worship truly. This view was crystalized by Puritan lawyer John Winthrop in his famous 1630 sermon delivered at Holyrood Church in Southampton, when he referred to their new Puritan community as "a city upon a hill," borrowing from Jesus' Sermon on the Mount in Matthew 5:14.[3] Consequently, historian George Marsden comments, "for better or for worse, mixes of religion and politics have always been one part of the American political heritage."[4]

Today, as historians take an honest look at the uglier side of American history, it is difficult to believe that America is uniquely privileged by God. It has long been a nation beset by slavery, violence, economic injustice, racism, corruption, and political division, to name but a few of its vices—hardly the picture of a godly paradise. Nevertheless, the cultural belief that America is God's special nation has endured. Challenging this belief by pointing out the historic ungodliness of American culture often ends up strengthening the prevailing opinion. If America seems anything but blessed, this is because she has strayed from her God, which is all the more reason to fight to restore the Christian heritage of this promised land. Only by returning to God, it is claimed, will America fulfill its promise as God's holy nation on earth. Indeed, Winthrop's "city upon a hill" imagery was also intended to inspire his hearers to live up to its ideals: "The image of a city upon a hill is, for Winthrop, the image of *preeminent responsibility*."[5]

According to American evangelical Jim Wallis, Abraham Lincoln got it right. We should not assume that God is on our side and invoke his name to bless whatever we think is important. "Rather, Lincoln said, we should pray and worry earnestly whether we are on God's side."[6] Wallis extrapolates on the importance of the distinction: "Those are the two ways that religion has been brought into public life in American history. The first way—God on our side—leads inevitably to triumphalism, self-righteousness, bad theology, and, often, dangerous foreign policy. The second way—asking if we are on God's side—leads to much healthier things, namely, penitence and even repentance, humility, reflection, and even accountability. We need much more of all these, because these are often the missing values of politics."[7]

American Christian belief typically assumes that cultural and political reform ought to move in a godward direction. And this is only natural. If we believe that something is good and right, we frequently believe it is good and right for everyone. The real question is to what extent American Christians should make cultural and political change a priority. Should the Christianization of American culture be the highest priority of their cultural engagement? As this chapter will argue, I believe American Christianity has missed the mark. Instead of pursuing cultural and political transformation of a nation, Christians ought to prioritize several other goals instead. And it is important that Christians reflect on the means of their influence.

FAITH AND POLITICS

Abortion, same-sex marriage, prayer in schools, religious freedom, creation versus evolution—these are but a few issues within American culture that evangelicals have worked tirelessly to influence. All of these issues have political manifestations, since it is understood that political influence is a powerful tool to shape culture. For decades evangelicals have believed "that they have a special role to play in keeping America Christian," as Du Mez has observed.[8] In the 1950s, evangelicals found themselves with access to the political mainstream—two decades before the Religious Right was born. Du Mez notes, "By the end of the decade, evangelicals had become active participants in national politics and had secured access to the highest levels of power."[9] But confidence in political influence has been a major misstep of American Christians, and of white evangelicals in particular. In an effort to impose Christian values on the wider society through political means, evangelicalism has become politicized to the extent that its spiritual nature has been distorted. The politicization of evangelicalism has damaged the credibility of the evangelical church. Historian Thomas Kidd comments, "White evangelicals' uncritical fealty to the GOP is real, and that fealty has done so much damage to the movement that it is uncertain whether the term *evangelical* can be rescued from its political and racial connotations."[10]

At the heart of this misstep is the assumption that political power will necessarily lead to transformation in American culture. But this assumption has been challenged in recent years. Sociologist James Davison Hunter has argued that cultural transformation rarely if ever happens through political mobilization. Rather, "cultural change is most enduring when it penetrates the structure of our imagination, frameworks of knowledge and discussion, the perception of everyday reality."[11] Political engagement is not wrong, but it is not a silver bullet to cultural transformation and renewal. Americans will live Christianly if they think Christianly, and that will happen only if their hearts are transformed by Christ. Laws do not transform hearts. Even less so political parties. For all its investment of capital, energy, and cultural disruption, evangelical political power has not led to a widespread turn to biblical values in America. If anything, through an overreliance on political power as the solution, evangelicalism has undermined its potential to bless society. And so Jim Wallis asks, "How did the faith of Jesus come to be known as pro-rich, pro-war, and only pro-American?"[12] To many today, evangelicals are perceived as politically power-hungry, guntoting, Trump-supporting white nationalists, and their ability to speak of Christ's message of reconciliation, peace, love, and equality is muted by other messages.

Trumpism

Historian John Fea put his finger on the issue when he wrote, "Trump's appeal to evangelical voters during the 2016 Republican primaries continues to baffle political commentators. How did a crude-talking, thrice-married, self-proclaimed philanderer and ultra-materialistic businessman who showed virtually no evidence of a Spirit-filled life win over evangelicals in a field of qualified GOP candidates who self-identified—in one way or another—with this form of conservative Christianity?"[13]

Donald Trump's 2020 reelection campaign garnered the support of 84 percent of self-identified white evangelicals (an increase from the 77 percent who voted for Trump in 2016).[14] Evangelicals were willing to overlook Christian values such as good character, honesty, and respect for others to win an election. So Du Mez observes,

> But evangelical support for Trump was no aberration, nor was it merely a pragmatic choice. It was, rather, the culmination

of evangelicals' embrace of militant masculinity, an ideology that enshrines patriarchal authority and condones the callous display of power, at home and abroad. By the time Trump arrived proclaiming himself their savior, conservative white evangelicals had already traded a faith that privileges humility and elevates "the least of these" for one that derides gentleness as the province of wusses. . . . In 2016, many observers were stunned at evangelicals' apparent betrayal of their own values. In reality, evangelicals did not cast their vote despite their beliefs, but because of them.[15]

Trump's first term had made it clear the kind of leader he was, but for many evangelicals, the opportunity to put Supreme Court justices on the bench, concerns about religious liberty, and the need to push against the liberal left agenda overcame any resistance they had to supporting Trump himself. Though he had publicly made racist and misogynistic statements and had a habit of repeated lying, they chose him to preserve political power. As Fea quips, "Character simply didn't matter as much as the opportunity to seize a seat on the Supreme Court."[16] Even after the storming of the Capitol on January 6, 2021, many white evangelicals remained steadfastly supportive of Trump.

What kind of message does this support send to the world? Many have noted the hypocrisy of the very same people who decried Bill Clinton's moral indiscretions—because "character matters!"—now endorsing a twice-divorced, adulterous, misogynistic woman abuser. Following the Lewinsky affair, Phyllis Schlafly wrote of the Clinton administration, "At stake is whether the White House will become a public relations vehicle for lying and polling, akin to a television show, or will remain a platform for the principled articulation of policies and values that Americans respect."[17] In an ironic twist, Schlafly later endorsed Trump for president, a man as infamous for his lying as for his reality TV show. James Dobson was another evangelical leader who was also appalled by Clinton's actions, stating that "character *does* matter. . . . You can't run a family, let alone a country without it."[18] Yet Dobson later endorsed Trump, who was ranked by C-SPAN's Presidential Historians Survey 2021 as the worst US president in history with regard to moral authority.[19] Evangelical theologian Wayne Grudem signed a public letter lambasting Clinton for "ill use of women" and "manipulation of truth."[20] Yet Grudem later endorsed Trump, even after Trump, in his book *The Art of the Deal*, bragged about bedding multiple married women. Jonathan Merritt comments, "Conservative evangelicals were unwilling to offer forgiveness to a Democrat who asked for it. But they have freely offered it to a Republican who doesn't want it."[21]

Some evangelicals have defended Trump on the grounds that he was a modern-day Cyrus—the Persian ruler who effected God's will for Israel, though he himself did not worship the God of Israel. This defense acknowledges that Trump is no real believer—despite the ludicrous claims of a few prominent "evangelicals," such as Paula White—but says he could effect God's will anyway. In confirmation of this theory, some have appealed to a correlation between Isaiah *45*—a chapter that describes Cyrus as God's chosen instrument—with Trump's status as the *45th* president.[22] Others have pointed to Israel's king David, who also committed adultery, yet was God's chosen king and forerunner to Jesus Christ himself. But they neglect to consider that when David was confronted with his sin in 2 Samuel 12, he was overcome with grief and repentance, as Psalm 51, which David wrote, so vividly records. Trump, on the other hand, has proudly declared that he has no reason to ask for God's forgiveness.

Evangelical support of Trump also communicates what evangelicals really care about—or, perhaps more important, what they don't care about. Data reveals that white evangelicals "support preemptive war, condone the use of torture, and favor the death penalty" more than any other religious demographic in America.[23] Evangelicals are more likely to own a gun, more opposed to immigration reform, and more likely to support Trump's border wall.[24] Yet many people—even many within the evangelical camp—find it difficult to reconcile such attitudes with Jesus' message. According to Jim Wallis, "The religious and political Right get the public meaning of religion mostly wrong—preferring to focus only on sexual and cultural issues while ignoring the weightier matters of justice."[25]

While some Trump-voting evangelicals might object that they do care about issues of social justice, this typically translates to one of two concerns that take priority over others. No political party is perfect, nor is any president, and many Christians have legitimate conscience problems voting the other way too. Nevertheless, there is a real choice to be made, and many chose to side with Trump despite his blatant lying, bullying, and incitement of hate. As Robert Jeffress, pastor of First Baptist Church, Dallas, quipped before the 2016 presidential election, "I want the meanest, toughest son-of-a-you-know-what I can find in that role, and I think that's where many evangelicals are."[26]

Mass Media

Hand in hand with efforts toward political influence is the evangelical harnessing of mass media. This impulse originated with fundamentalists who wanted the 1925 Scopes Trial to become "a journalistic extravaganza."[27] But the impulse can backfire, as it did with Scopes. After the farcical nature of the trial, in which William Jennings Bryan failed to make a biblical case for his anti-evolution cause, fundamentalists "became stereotyped as buffoonish southern bumpkins."[28]

Yet media has also been used to promote the evangelical cause, as observed in Ross Douthat's description of Billy Graham's influence: "Little more than a generation passed between the Scopes Monkey Trial and the great Manhattan crusade of 1957, but it might as well have been an eternity. With his command of mass media, his television broadcasts and stadium appearances and global tours, Billy Graham had done the near-impossible: he had carried Evangelical Christianity from the margins to the mainstream, making Evangelical faith seem respectable as well as fervent, not only relevant but *modern*."[29]

To this day, media remains an essential ingredient of evangelical engagement, with countless TV shows, films, radio programs, music, literature, social media, and podcasts employed to further the evangelical social agenda. Some have criticized these efforts, noting that evangelical engagement with the arts is sometimes shallow or poorly done. Douthat comments that much of "evangelical art and architecture [is] generally middlebrow, garish, and naive" and its pop culture "ingenuous and tacky—the stuff of Kirk Cameron movies and Christian rock music, geared to an undemanding audience and easily dismissed by anyone outside the circle of the devout."[30] And another part of the problem is an overreliance on impersonal forms of media to get the work of gospel proclamation done. Christianity is centered on a message about Jesus Christ, and believers are commissioned to share that message with others. Naturally, mass media is a way that message can be conveyed to large audiences. But evangelicals sometimes fail to recognize that mass media has limitations and might not fully accomplish the goals of Christian proclamation. If a key purpose of proclamation is to transform hearts, mass media might not be an effective means to that end. It may be part of the process; it may generate interest; it may stimulate thought and conversation; but rarely has anyone decided to follow Jesus because of a post on Twitter. And those few who do still require a believing community to embrace and encourage them and to equip them with the basics of the Christian faith. That does not happen in a meaningful or lasting way through many forms of media. It happens through relationships with real people in the church. In this regard, evangelical faith in media is misplaced, in much the same way that faith in political influence is misplaced.

Evangelical overconfidence in the ability of politics and media to bring spiritual transformation doesn't mean evangelicalism fails entirely. It is certainly a force to be reckoned with and now has the ability to influence the outcome of presidential races. By that measure, it is a successful religious faction with real societal power. But at what cost? Does this success translate to significant gains for the cause of Christ in America? According to historian Thomas Kidd, "The Scopes Trial illustrated the temptations of media access, establishmentarian politics, and celebrity politicians in evangelical history. That combination of power politics and media imagery accounts for much of the crisis evangelicals are facing today."[31]

MOMS AND GUNS

Trumpism is a relatively new phenomenon, but evangelicals have been politically active for decades. And while Trump represents a crisis of evangelical politicization, we should also consider the movement's long-standing political causes. Of these, there has been no greater evangelical burden than opposition to abortion, which Kidd describes as "the single most important issue to many white evangelical voters."[32]

Abortion

The anti-abortion cause has not always attracted the attention of evangelical voters. It was once the purview of the American Catholic Church, but evangelicals joined their cause after *Roe v. Wade* and pursued relentless political opposition to legalized abortion after that defining moment of American history.[33] The fight against abortion became a powerful political movement within evangelicalism, with many single-issue voters casting their ballots in opposition to abortion regardless of a politician's other policies and leadership flaws.

It is difficult to critique the stance against abortion from a biblical perspective. There is strong biblical concern for the dignity of human life and the protection of the defenseless, and this alone makes most abortions abhorrent to believers. Conversely, it is difficult to defend "a mother's right to choose" from the Bible. Evangelical and Catholic opposition to abortion is entirely warranted. The question, however, is whether one's political decisions should be driven by a single issue—and one issue only. Though many evangelicals have thrown support behind four Republican presidential administrations since *Roe v.*

Wade, for fifty years those political efforts failed to overturn that decision. What about the other policies that single-issue evangelicals have unwittingly supported in opposing abortion? Such policies received votes in the name of overturning *Roe v. Wade*, and now that that goal has been realized, we might ask, At what cost?

In addition, there is the problem we looked at earlier: an overconfidence in political power. Now that *Roe v. Wade* has been overturned, will that stop women from seeking abortions? Or will it just increase the number of mother-and-child deaths through unsafe illegal abortions? Perhaps persuasion would be more effective than legislation in reducing abortions, along with stronger measures to protect women from rape and sexual abuse. Greater provision of material support and care for pregnant women would also help. Easier pathways to adoption might help too. The evangelical focus on media could be harnessed to argue for the sanctity of human life not for political purposes but to persuade mothers to love the child within. Minimally, evangelicals need to consider whether the outcome they seek can best be accomplished by political means or if there are better ways to oppose abortion than through politics.

Recent research has demonstrated that the abortion rate in the United States fell to its lowest level ever in 2018—even lower than the rate preceding *Roe v. Wade* in 1973.[34] Globally, data show that "stricter abortion laws do not lead to fewer abortions" and that "preventing unwanted pregnancies has a significant effect on reducing the number of terminations."[35] Research demonstrates that the most effective strategy to reduce abortion rates is to increase access to contraception.[36] If we take it as a given that lowering the number of terminations is the goal, perhaps evangelicals should give more weight to strategies besides making abortion illegal.

Finally, I urge political evangelicals to change their focus now that *Roe v. Wade* has been overturned. If the protection of unborn children has been their driving force, now they have a responsibility to protect those children who will be born rather than aborted. We may see greater demand for foster care, adoption, provision of basic necessities, and schooling for unwanted children. I trust that evangelicals will throw as much energy and resources behind such needs as they did to overturn *Roe v. Wade*. And having dodged the bullet of abortion, surely these children should not have to live in fear of being gunned down by an AR-15 on a school day.

Guns

As an Australian Christian in America, I found American evangelical support of gun ownership was an instant culture clash for me. Many non-American evangelicals find it difficult to understand and accept why their American counterparts are so supportive of the right to bear arms. When I lived in the United States, Christians' attitude toward guns was a hot-trigger issue, and while we might have agreed on most things, we just couldn't see eye to eye on guns. A beloved member of a church small-group Bible study that I led once revealed that he was carrying a gun at our small group meeting. No one else seemed to think it was a big deal, but I did. And apparently he had been asked to bring his gun to church every Sunday in case something happens. I was flabbergasted.

That America has a gun problem is self-evident. There are more guns than people in America. Americans own nearly half of all civilian-owned guns in the world. They own more guns per capita than residents of any other country, with more than double the nearest competition (Yemen). And saddest of all, gun homicide rates are twenty-five times higher in the United States than in other high-income countries.[37] There are more mass shootings in America than anywhere else, and according to many American evangelicals the solution is not fewer guns but more. I had the same conversation several times, and the argument unfolds as follows. There are millions of guns out there already. If Americans were to restrict gun ownership, only law-abiding citizens would obey. And that means that the bad guys would keep their guns while the good guys would become defenseless against them. This logic makes sense—to a point. I understand there are no simple solutions to the problem, but it seems questionable that more guns is the answer. I understand the importance of the Second Amendment to many Americans. Bearing arms is seen as necessary to resist tyranny and the removal of natural rights. But these are, fundamentally, American concerns, not universal Christian concerns.

The problem I wish to raise here is that some American evangelicals fail to see the difference between their American values and their Christian ones. These values are conflated so that an affront to Americanism is now an affront to Christianity. In this way of thinking, questioning the contemporary need for the Second Amendment is as un-Christian as it is un-American.

THE TWO KINGDOMS

The tensions raised by the conflation of American values with Christian values lead to bigger questions. How should Christians relate to the state? What is the role of faith in politics? Does evangelical commitment mandate partisan loyalty? Or as Jim Wallis asks, "Dare we search for the politics of God? It's much easier to just use God to justify our politics."[38] Discussion about these issues spans millennia, and I won't attempt to resolve the complexity of those questions here. What I will offer, however, is a short biblical framework to help tackle some of them.

The Otherworldly Kingdom

The basic framework presented by Jesus and the New Testament is that of two kingdoms. While many of Jesus' followers expected the promised Messiah to be a political leader who would overthrow Israel's Roman oppressors, Jesus repeatedly denied this understanding of his mission. He was the promised Messiah, yes. And messianic expectation was earthly in scope. But Jesus would not overthrow Rome, at least not in the way his followers expected. He would not lead a political rebellion. He would not seek a merely earthly kingdom at all. When Pontius Pilate asked Jesus if he was the king of the Jews (John 18:33), Jesus told Pilate that his kingdom is not of this world (v. 36). Literally, he says his kingdom is not "from this world," indicating that "Jesus' kingdom is not grounded in this world or established by means of this world," according to biblical scholar Edward Klink.[39] If his kingdom were earthly in origin, his followers would fight for him. But because his kingdom originates from another place, his followers do not act according to the rules of earth-born kingdoms, which operate with armed might (v. 36).[40] Rather, their behavior is informed by the nature of Jesus' otherworldly kingdom.

The apostle Paul put a sharper edge on this contrast when he told the Colossians that God "has rescued us from the dominion of darkness and brought us into the kingdom of the Son he loves" (Colossians 1:13). Here we see two kingdoms in opposition to each other. The dominion of darkness is as bad as it sounds, and people caught up in it require God's rescue. And it is also clear that this dominion does not refer to a particular empire or earthly kingdom. It is, according to biblical scholar Scot McKnight, "the deep, cosmic demonic personal realities capturing structures and society and people in this world systematically to thwart the good plan of God."[41] Our world is subjected to darkness, ruled by shady overlords who oppress its subjects and keep them captive. The Roman Empire was subjected to that darkness. The Ottoman Empire was subjected to that darkness. And dare I say it, the United States of America is subjected to that darkness. By claiming this, I do not mean to say that America is evil—at least, it is no more so than other empires. I just mean that America is part of the world, which is itself subjected to the dominion of darkness, according to Paul.

Believers, however, are rescued from the dominion of darkness and have been brought into the kingdom of God's Son. This is the kingdom that Jesus spoke about to Pilate. It is a kingdom not of this world. It is a spiritual kingdom, ruled by Jesus himself, which sets its subjects free from darkness through redemption and the forgiveness of sins (Colossians 1:14). Every true believer in Jesus has been transferred out of their native kingdom of darkness and now belongs to the one ruled by him.[42] While genuine believers no longer belong to the world ruled by darkness, they nevertheless continue to live in it. On the eve of his crucifixion, Jesus prayed about his followers, acknowledging that "they are not of the world any more than I am of the world" (John 17:14). He continued, "My prayer is not that you take them out of the world but that you protect them from the evil one" (v. 15). This is why believers often say they are *in* the world but not *of* the world. They live in this world, which is still subjected to the dominion of darkness, but they do not belong to it. They belong to Jesus' kingdom, which is not of this world. Peter expresses a similar idea when he addresses his readers as "foreigners and exiles" in the world (1 Peter 2:11). On the one hand, they are to live as good citizens in their earthly situation, including submitting "to every human authority: whether to the emperor, as the supreme authority, or to governors" (vv. 13–14). They are *in* the world. But as "foreigners and exiles," or as "sojourners," believers do not regard the world as their home. They are not of the world. Their home is a future world.[43]

Disentangling Allegiances

What does all this mean for understanding Christian involvement in politics? How are God and country related? And what does this relationship mean for Christian involvement in the culture wars? Evangelicals may argue about the specifics, but the big picture is clear: believers belong to the kingdom of Christ, which does not originate from this world. Australia *does* originate from this world. China originates from this world. America originates from this world. But Jesus' kingdom does not originate from this world. As theologian Oliver O'Donovan writes, "There is only one society which is incorporated into the Kingdom of God . . . and that is the church."[44] When Christians say that America is God's country, or that we are called to turn America into Christ's kingdom, we betray a serious misunderstanding of the Bible. Jesus has not given his followers a mandate to turn earthly political kingdoms into the kingdom of Christ. Do we really think we can establish Jesus' kingdom through meager political activism when Jesus died and rose again to bring his kingdom?

This should not be taken to mean that Christians should avoid engaging in politics or culture at all. Believers have every right to engage, create, and help to shape the culture and the country in which they live. Being a good foreign resident in the world means that we should obey the authorities (as far as possible) and, if we're given an opportunity, shape that authority in ways that seek the good of others. Knowledge of the crucified and vindicated Christ allows believers to offer Jesus-shaped substance to inform society's understanding of justice, freedom, peace, and truth.[45] But we should never believe the lie that we can, or ever will, turn a worldly culture into the kingdom of Christ. Not only is that impossible but it disrespects Jesus' teaching and his mission. The Old Testament reveals a God who frequently addresses politics, speaking "about what believing in God means in this world (not just the next one), about faith and 'public life' (not just private piety), about our responsibilities for the common good (not just for our own private religious experience)."[46] The prophets often spoke about "political" subjects such as "land, labor, capital, wages, debt, taxes, equity, fairness, courts, prisons, immigrants, other races and peoples, economic divisions, social justice, war, and peace."[47] But the New Testament introduces a shift, where the locus of God's activity is through the church. Jesus does not advocate political activism for the establishment of his kingdom, nor does he endorse political power as the means to achieve kingdom purposes. Instead, believers are instructed to obey the authorities (1 Peter 2:13–14; Romans 13:1–7) and to pray for them (1 Timothy 2:1–2). While the pursuit of political office is not prohibited, it is odd that many evangelicals today

29

believe that the primary way they can do God's work is to win elections and support partisan priorities. This belief often prevents them from doing what God *has* called them to do.

Being Salt and Light

Jesus told his followers they were the salt of the earth and the light of the world (Matthew 5:13–14). He did not say they needed to *become* salt or light. They already are salt and light. But these statements of fact come with exhortations too: the salt must not lose its saltiness (v. 13), and the light must be allowed to shine before others (v. 16). If the salt loses its saltiness, it's irreversibly rendered useless (v. 13). And light is likewise useless if it is hidden or covered (v. 15). Two outcomes are imagined here—one negative and one positive. The negative outcome is that no longer salty salt will be "thrown out and trampled underfoot" (v. 13). The positive outcome, however, is that shining light allows others to "see your good deeds and glorify your Father in heaven" (v. 16). Clearly, followers of Jesus are not meant to be useless in this world. They're not to be "too heavenly minded for any earthly good." They're supposed to add value to the world they live in. And notice how this should happen: through good deeds.

Good deeds should not need to be explained, but here's a hint as to how we will recognize them: people will "glorify your Father in heaven" when they see your good deeds (v. 16). This expresses "a way of being in the world that is visible as deeds and dispositions that honor the disciples' Heavenly Father," according to biblical scholar Jonathan Pennington.[48] Good deeds point others to God's goodness. Political partisanship, often accompanied by hate-filled rhetoric, will never lead anyone to glorify

God. Inciting violence, hatred, and division does not point others to God's goodness. Rather, these activities lead others to despise Christians and the church.

Jim Wallis, writing in 2005, tells an interesting Tale of Two Movements about the two major faith-inspired movements of the previous fifty years: the Black-church-led civil-rights movement of the 1950s and '60s, and the Religious Right movement of the 1980s and '90s as exemplified by Jerry Falwell's Moral Majority and Pat Robertson's Christian Coalition.[49] Wallis observes that the civil-rights advocates "built a movement that was morally based and politically independent." Its strength and base were not inside politics but at the grassroots, and this was the key to its success: "The movement changed the way the American people *thought* about race and sought to affect the very cultural values of the country."[50] The Religious Right, on the other hand, "went for political power right away," trying "to take over the Republican Party and then implement their legislative agenda." But "the critical step of persuading by moral argument . . . was neglected."[51] In the end, the civil-rights movement was far more powerful and influential by operating "out of its spiritual strength and letting its political influence flow from its moral influence." In this way, it took its cue from other great causes led by religious communities, such as the abolition of slavery, child-labor reform, and women's suffrage—all of which exemplified the same strategy.[52]

Making Disciples

Jesus' final instruction, recorded in Matthew's Gospel, is known as the Great Commission: "Therefore go and make disciples of all nations, baptizing them in the name of the Father and of the

31

Son and of the Holy Spirit, and teaching them to obey everything I have commanded you" (Matthew 28:19–20). Throughout the ages, the church has regarded the Great Commission as one of the most important instructions that Jesus gave to believers (hence its name), and it has inspired countless individuals to leave their comfort zones to reach others in Jesus' name. As Mark Dever says, "The Christian life is the discipled life and the discipling life."[53] Evangelicals are passionate about the Great Commission, to be sure. Evangelicals want to make disciples of all nations. They want to see them baptized in the name of the Father, Son, and Holy Spirit. They want to pass on all that Jesus taught. The trouble is that today's culture wars and political partisanship have greatly compromised their ability to fulfill the Great Commission.

Jesus commissioned his followers to make disciples of all nations, not disciples of a political party. He commissioned his followers to baptize in his name, not to win the White House. The irony is that by prioritizing victory in a cultural war, today's evangelicals have compromised their ability to fulfill Jesus' commission, having lost credibility and moral standing in the public square. By fighting for political influence no matter the cost, evangelicals are no longer viewed as trustworthy arbiters of spiritual truth. They are seen not as Jesus' representatives in the world but as power-hungry, self-interested hypocrites.

In his book *God in the White House*, historian Randall Balmer concludes, "My reading of American religious history is that religion always functions best from the margins of society and not in the councils of power. Once you identify the faith with a particular candidate or party or with the quest for political influence, *ultimately it is the faith that suffers*."[54] Evangelicals have repeated this history and fulfilled its prophecy. In contrast, ethicist David Gushee outlines "Seven Marks of Healthy Christian Politics," which offer a healthy starting point for a distinctly Christian engagement in the political realm:

- A distinctive Christian identity, not a civil religion.
- A politics of hope, not fear.
- Critical distance from all earthly powers, not partisanship, partnership, or surrender.
- A discipline provided by a Christian social teaching tradition, not ideology or improv.
- A global perspective, not parochial or nationalist.
- A vision for the common good, not the church's self-interest.
- A people who practice what they preach, not hypocrites or load-shifters.[55]

Christian political activity should be marked by godly character and prophetic conviction, rather than partisan loyalty and the pursuit of power.

BE LIKE THE EARLY CHURCH

The early church faced challenges similar to the Western church today. Like our own, the Roman Empire was a pluralistic and relativistic society. As in our culture, sexual freedom and self-fulfillment were highly valued.[56] And Rome was hostile to Christians and their message in ways that are increasingly similar to the hostility we see in the West today. We're not yet at the stage of arresting, torturing, and executing Christians as the Romans did, but that does happen in some parts of the world today and may be true of the West in due course.

Yet in its first three centuries, the church flourished throughout the Roman Empire. And this was not because Emperor Constantine converted to Christianity in AD 312. Rather, it was the other way around. Christianity had grown so popular by that time that it was politically expedient for Constantine to convert.[57] Helen Rhee comments, "When Constantine seized the imperial power with the power of the Christian God, the church had been functioning as a formidable social and economic institution with massive operation of charity."[58] So what accounts for the massive growth of Christianity before 312?

By all accounts, Christianity grew because Christians loved their neighbors.[59] While Roman religion discouraged helping the poor—because they must have offended the gods and therefore deserved to suffer, and because pity was regarded as a character defect[60]—Christians cared for those in need.[61] Christians comforted the outcasts, the widows, and the orphans. Many Christians gladly risked their lives and died by serving highly contagious victims of the plague, whom no one else would even touch.[62] Christians were known for loving their enemies, even while they were regularly persecuted through imprisonment, torture, and death.

Before AD 312, there was nothing political about the early church.[63] Those first Christians did not try to get "their people" into powerful positions of governance. They did not try to change laws in their favor. They did not try to legislate Christian belief. They simply went about their business being salt and light in the world and making disciples of all nations. And their good deeds commended them to the skeptics around them. Christians became so well known for their care of the poor that Emperor Julian the Apostate lamented in AD 362 how they made the Romans look bad: "For it is disgraceful that, when . . . the impious Galilaeans [Christians] support not only their own poor but ours as well, all men see that our people lack aid from us."[64]

The early Christians were deeply countercultural in their beliefs and practices. They worshiped a crucified God who rose from the dead, and they loved the poor and marginalized. The Romans struggled to understand such a strange "superstition" because it was so different from anything they had ever known. And yet by the beginning of the fourth century, Christianity had become a major cultural force within the empire. But its influence came through Christians' love and good deeds, not through political action. Christianity's later political influence came as a result of Christians' affecting people's hearts and minds, not the other way around.

Evangelicals today should learn from the early church's example. When faced with a choice between achieving a spiritual good through political power or loving our neighbors through good deeds, believers should prioritize Jesus' means and methods. We should relinquish the false hope of winning the culture through political discipleship and focus on making disciples of Jesus. Christians should be known less for self-seeking political fervor and famous for our service to others. In these ways, evangelicals will again bring glory to God. And—who knows?—they might actually win over the culture without trying.

EXCLUSION ZONES

Love your enemies and pray for
those who persecute you.

THE MESSAGE OF CHRIST IS AN OPEN INVITATION TO ALL PEOPLE to know God, to experience redemption, and to enter the eternal love of Jesus. Yet repeatedly, evangelicals find reasons to keep outsiders on the outside.

In America, the oldest stimulus of exclusion is race. While white evangelicalism provided impetus to the abolition movement, at the same time it empowered slavery and the ensuing racial divisions that have plagued American culture to this day. Even now, issues of racial justice polarize evangelicals and exclude marginalized people groups.

Evangelicals often also treat homosexuality and transgenderism as stimuli of exclusion, largely because of evangelical opposition to same-sex marriage and gender diversity, which has recently been a brutal frontline battle within a larger ongoing culture war. Regardless of how individual Christians might relate to homosexual or transgender individuals, the perception is that evangelicalism is not a safe space for such people. Rightly or wrongly, evangelicals must reckon with the reality that they are perceived as intolerant, judgmental, and exclusivist.

These "exclusion zones" are not unique to American evangelicalism, of course. In Australia, same-sex marriage became legally recognized in December 2017 following a national postal survey designed to gauge support for the change to marriage legislation. The national debate over the issue was probably the most negative thing to happen to the perception of evangelicalism in a generation. This was partly because of clever marketing from the gay and lesbian movement, whose slogan "Love is love" was very difficult to argue against. But evangelicals also made some blunders. The most prominent example is the Anglican Diocese of Sydney's donation of one million dollars to the same-sex marriage "No" campaign.[1] Regardless of what motivated the donation, the message the gay and lesbian community received was that evangelical Anglicans are opposed to them. They are excluded from the church. They are the enemy. Moreover, the matter reinforced national stereotypes that evangelicals are intolerant and opposed to love. Even if the No campaign had successfully delayed same-sex marriage in Australia, it would have been a net loss for evangelicals, causing even fewer people to want to have anything to do with them, let alone convert. As it was, evangelicals not only failed to delay same-sex marriage but lost significant public esteem as well, damaging their witness to Christ.

Keeping groups on the margins is less noticeable when numbers are in your favor. But with the increased secularization of

Western societies, evangelicals are rapidly losing that advantage. At the same time, marginalized groups are growing in prominence. So what happens when the marginalized become less marginal? To begin, the oppressive majority undergoes public judgment. That's exactly what's happening to evangelicals. While Christians were once regarded as good citizens, they are increasingly viewed as hateful, evil people. One of the reasons that evangelicals are increasingly being pushed to the margins of society is because the groups they once marginalized are on the ascendancy.

THE OUTSIDERS

Whether or not it is intended, evangelicals' posture toward marginalized groups is perceived as "us versus them." "They" are excluded. "They" are the outsiders. "They" are the enemy. In many respects, that is an unfair characterization. Countless evangelicals gladly affirm that God loves all people, regardless of their sexual orientation, gender diversity, or race. Such evangelicals also seek to love all people in their personal interactions and relationships.

But as evangelicals are increasingly viewed as a voting bloc, as a political lobby group, and as culture warriors, their message of love for all people is muted by their opposition to outsiders' versions of justice and the good life. The "us versus them" mentality that characterizes the way many evangelicals think and respond to others is alive and well among evangelicals of all stripes—theological, cultural, and political. And it undermines the message of Christ.

Sexuality

Besides American evangelicals' unflinching political support of Donald Trump, no issue has put American evangelicals in a more negative light than opposition to same-sex marriage, which has solidified the perception that evangelicals are homophobic and opposed to freedom and love. Those outside the evangelical world see this opposition as moralistic, cruel, and antiquated. They accuse evangelicals of trying to force their beliefs on the rest of society.

To be sure, there is widespread misunderstanding about what evangelicals believe about homosexuality and same-sex marriage. It is popular to dismiss conservative Christian views on the basis that some verse on sexuality in Leviticus is apparently upheld, while no Christian today upholds the verses in the same book about not eating pork. This is the "Josiah Bartlet argument," immortalized by America's best fictional president on the TV show *The West Wing* when he excoriated an evangelical for her opposition to homosexuality. But evangelical views are generally more sophisticated than simply cherry-picking verses out of context. First, many evangelicals have promoted a broader, positive argument about the design and intention of marriage, a fundamental first step (Genesis 2; Ephesians 5:22–33).[2] Second, it is wrong to assume that only the Old Testament contains challenging texts about homosexuality. The New Testament has plenty to say on the subject as well (Romans 1:18–32). Suffice it to say, Christians differ on the interpretation and application of the relevant texts, and this is not the place to weigh in on those discussions.[3] Regardless of their theological position, there are aspects of how evangelicals communicate their message that they would do well to think more carefully about.

The most prevalent argument among evangelicalism's critics is that marriage does not belong to Christians exclusively. Who are we to insist on what is and is not marriage? While it is true that marriage does not *belong* to Christians, that's not how most Christians view it. If you believe that God is the creator of marriage and that his intention is for human flourishing and the formation of families around a husband-and-wife relationship, then you also believe that this is true and good for everyone, whether or not they are believers. I agree that God is the creator of marriage and that he intended it for our common good. But this also means it is a gift of creation for all people—like the sun. In this sense, Christians can no more claim that marriage belongs to us than we can claim to own the sun. If that's true, then why do Christians insist on defining the rules of marriage for everyone else?

The second argument against evangelical opposition to same-sex marriage follows from the first. As long as two consenting adults are involved, why do evangelicals care if they choose to be together and call that marriage? There is no parallel in this case to the issue of abortion, a matter in which innocent lives are at stake and require protection. Adults can make their own decisions and no one else is harmed. If these adults do not share evangelical convictions about God and creation, it is hardly surprising that they will hold views about marriage different from most evangelicals as well. The point here is that adults are free to think and do what they want, regardless of whether evangelicals believe their thinking is mistaken.

Most evangelicals respond by arguing that the institution of marriage is bigger than the individuals who participate in it. And that institution exists to create a legal space in society to recognize, regulate, and reify a biological relationship that gives rise to a family in which children are naturally engendered and legally recognized as the offspring of their biological parents. But critics quickly respond that not all marriages do this, as in cases of infertility and adoption, and the institution is not fundamentally altered or undermined by this reality. In the same way, gay marriage need not alter nor undermine the institution of marriage, despite evangelical protestations to the contrary.

Others will argue that the traditional nuclear family is the foundation of society and that therefore the common good is at stake if the traditional family unit is degraded by same-sex marriage. But considering that same-sex marriages account for less than one half of one percent of marriages in the United States, this might be seen as an overreaction.[4] Same-sex marriage is not prevalent enough to undermine the traditional family's role as the foundation of society.

A third common argument against evangelical opposition to same-sex marriage is rooted in evangelical misunderstandings of Romans 1:18–32 and how that passage is used. This passage views homosexuality as an outworking of a fractured knowledge of God. But homosexuality is a symptom, not a cause, and the passage does not address individuals and their choices. Instead, it paints a picture of societies and cultures as they move farther away from God, and whose trajectory is largely set.[5] Attempts to halt the outworking of this judgment may find little success, and it could even be argued that evangelicals who try to impede the "outworking" of Romans 1:18–32 are opposing the plan of God, since these societies are experiencing the results of a fractured knowledge of God as an expression of his judgment.

In light of these objections, a case can be made that evangelical opposition to same-sex marriage—at least in a political context—will lead to little positive benefit and is most likely to further spoil evangelicals' image. Evangelicals should weigh whether it is worth spending what's left of their moral capital on this issue, especially now that same-sex marriage has become legal across the United States. The institution of marriage has survived this legalization, and the imagined worst-case scenarios have not come to pass. As far as I know, only one American has decided to marry their cat[6] (though Barbarella Buchner of Spain married her two cats eleven years ago).[7] Yes, the legalization of same-sex marriage places conservative Christians farther outside the accepted cultural norms, but that is hardly a reason to oppose it—at least, it is not a *Christian* reason to oppose it. The vibrancy and spiritual health of Christ's church do not depend on the church's social legitimacy. Church history suggests the opposite: when the church is accepted by mainstream society, it grows corrupt, and when the church is outside the mainstream, it flourishes. The church of the first few centuries did not attempt to enforce its sexual values on the Roman Empire. Granted, that would have been a futile exercise given that Christian morals were not widely accepted. But it likely would have dampened the positive witness the church achieved by loving social outcasts and their enemies. Perhaps if the evangelical church today focused more on doing this—loving their enemies and those ostracized by society—rather than opposing the sexual preferences of mainstream America, more people would be interested in what evangelicals have to say.

As evangelicals have become identified by their opposition to same-sex marriage, they have faced a communication problem. Mainstream society knows what evangelicals are against rather than what they are for. Christians should be known for their countercultural, self-sacrificial love as the best way to point others to God's love in Christ. When they are known instead for their opposition to same-sex marriage, they bear witness to a false god, one who is opposed to sexual deviants he couldn't possibly love. David Gushee testifies, "I have met gay people all over America for whom Christians and 'the church' were literally their most dangerous enemies. I have also known gay people who stood vigil over their dead friends when those friends' Christian families would not even deign to bury them."[8] How tragic.

Obviously, this is a complicated issue, especially for Christians who want to take the Bible seriously. Mainstream sexual ethics are at odds with a conservative understanding of the Scriptures, and Christians do not always agree on how to handle such issues.[9] As Gushee admits, "We do need to temper evangelical perfectionism with a loving realism about human nature and today's cultural realities. But we must not entirely lose contact with the wisdom of Scripture, history, and tradition."[10] At the risk of oversimplifying a complex issue, I would simply ask that all Christians take a step back from an "us versus them" mentality and look at the bigger picture. How we respond to issues of sexual diversity—and more important, how we relate to *people*—matters more than being right or imposing Christian values on others. As ambassadors of Christ, we must demonstrate love and acceptance. This should be the loudest message that people hear from the church. But that is rarely the case.

Gender

As though changing sexual norms were not enough to navigate, gender is now an additional challenge. Just staying abreast of the changes in language, labels, and gender jargon is difficult. Before grasping the nuances of transgenderism, gender fluidity, and gender dysphoria, we should understand that the term *gender* itself is fluid, depending on whether you're talking about biological sex, sex-based social structures, or gender identity. Before 1955, *gender* was used to refer to grammatical categories (masculine, feminine, and neuter nouns, etc.). But this began to change after sexologist John Money posited the distinction between biological sex and gender roles, which became widely accepted in the 1970s. Today, the term *gender* can exclude biological sex or include it, and in popular use it is often its synonym. The distinction some make between gender roles and biological sex, therefore, is often not properly understood at a popular level.

If it were not possible to distinguish gender from sex, the issue would be relatively straightforward, since sex is biologically determined. And many evangelicals assume that to be the case: since sex biologically determines gender, any confusion on the matter exists only in the mind of the individual. This assumption is imbibed from the Bible's apparent lack of distinction between gender and sex. And while it is true that the Bible—as an artifact of the ancient world—did not have a developed way of discussing the difference between gender and sex, there are nevertheless some hints of the distinction. For example, there is a "Christian" way for wives to relate to their husbands and vice versa (Ephesians 5:22–33; 1 Peter 3:1–7). While these Christian approaches to marriage bear strong parallels to the expectations of contemporary Greco-Roman culture, they are distinct in important ways. Specifically Christian gender roles within marriage differ from the gender roles of non-Christian marriages of the day. This difference indicates that there is some flexibility with how gender roles are conceived. If such roles were determined by biological sex, there could be no Christian way of being a husband or wife, since all gender roles would be fixed by biology, regardless of one's Christian commitment. That gender roles are culturally defined does not fully address gender dysphoria and transgenderism, but it does show that even the Bible—though it forbids Israelites from engaging in cross-dressing on the one hand (Deuteronomy 22:5)—is not as black and white on the topic of gender as many evangelicals assume.

Evangelicals tend to base their objections to both trans-genderism and homosexuality on two main points. They argue that neither transgenderism nor homosexuality is determined by biology and that both of these are contrary to God's design. If they are not determined by biology, it follows that people can "choose" how to be and live.[11] Together with the second point, this means that homosexuality and transgenderism are choices to reject God's design. Regarding biology, however, there is still debate as to the genetic predisposition toward homosexuality.[12] If it were to be demonstrated that some people have a genetic pre-disposition to homosexuality, it would undermine the first point of the argument. Biology is relied on to critique transgenderism as well, by asserting that a person's sex is fixed by virtue of their chromosomes, regardless of what sexual organs they have. But again, chromosomes speak to biological sex, not necessarily to gender expression. The appeal to biology works only if the distinction between sex and gender is rejected *a priori*.

Christians, of all people, should know that the human person is much more than the body.[13] As with sexual diversity, evangelicals need to think through the bigger picture of gender diversity. If someone experiences genuine gender dysphoria—believing that they were born the wrong sex—how will citing Deuteronomy 22:5 help them? How will pointing to the binary nature of male and female sexes prior to the fall of Genesis 3 assist them in that struggle? How will it help to tell them that their gender must be aligned with their biological sex or they are living contrary to God's design? How will an insistence on binary sexuality help someone struggling with the perplexing reality of intersex biology? Many evangelical answers to these questions come across as simplistic and insufficient to address the complex and disorienting realities of gender dysphoria. They lack mercy and only increase a person's sense of their brokenness and condemnation. Often it is best to begin by recognizing that those who experience gender dysphoria are not making a choice and that telling them to rectify something they have no control over does not help them. They might be able to resist cross-dressing to satisfy Deuteronomy 22:5 (and the Christian community), but that will do nothing to address their inner turmoil. They can pray for help, but prayer is not a guarantee that God will irrevocably reverse the situation. Paul prayed that God would remove the thorn in his flesh that tormented him—whatever that was—but was denied. Why? Because, as God told Paul, "My grace is sufficient for you, for my power is made perfect in weakness" (2 Corinthians 12:7–9). In place of simplistic solutions, evangelicals need to be prepared to offer grace and understanding to those who need it.

Race

In his book *Might from the Margins*, Dennis Edwards looks at the history of American Christianity and ponders, "In light of the toxicity of American Christianity, it's reasonable to wonder now, as Howard Thurman did back in the 1940s, why African Americans, or anyone on the margins of society, would become Christian."[14]

American Christianity has a long and complicated history of compromise on the matter of racial justice. The Southern Baptist Convention was formed in 1845 because of a dispute over whether a slaveholder could be commissioned as a missionary. Rather than acknowledge slavery to be sinful, three hundred Baptist leaders split from their northern Baptist counterparts to establish the new denomination.[15] The four founding faculty members of the Southern Baptist Seminary owned slaves and made theological defenses of slavery.[16] In the north, many evangelicals regarded slavery a great evil, but this often did not translate into Black equality.[17] In the early twentieth century, an ordained Baptist preacher led the revival of the Ku Klux Klan.[18] While Billy Graham invited Martin Luther King (both were Baptists) to give the opening prayer at one of his 1957 rallies,[19] white Southern evangelicals resisted the civil-rights movement led by Dr. King.[20] After the presidency of Barack Obama, laments David Gushee,[21] the Republicans "chose the most extreme white backlash candidate," backed by the majority of white evangelicals.

Yet despite American evangelicals' often mixed messaging to the contrary, the Bible is clear about God's vision for racial diversity. Jemar Tisby writes, "From beginning to end, from Genesis to Revelation, God has planned for a racially and ethnically diverse church."[22]

Diverse skin tones and cultures are a wonderful feature of God's creativity. No skin color is endowed with superiority, nor is one race of people to be privileged over others. All people are created in God's image and therefore share equally in the privilege of being the pinnacle of his creation (Genesis 1:26–27). Jesus sent his followers to make disciples of all nations—or literally, all peoples (Matthew 28:19). God loves all peoples and ethnic groups, and they will each be represented before his heavenly throne (Revelation 7:9).

I don't know any evangelicals today who would admit to being racist. But as Robert Jones writes, "Whatever the explicit public proclamations of white denominations and individual Christians, the public opinion data reveal that the historical legacy of white supremacy lives on in white Christianity today."[23] Though contemporary American evangelicals claim to oppose racism, they do not oppose racism in all of its forms. There continues to be widespread evangelical complicity in systems that oppress nonwhite people. As Tisby comments, "Racism can operate through impersonal systems and not simply through the malicious words and actions of individuals. . . . Christians participated in this system of white supremacy . . . even if they claim people of color as their brothers and sisters in Christ."[24] Many evangelicals often oppose or dismiss the very notion of systemic racism. They claim that they accept all people and that they do not have racist hearts. While this is a good start, it is not sufficient. It is an individualistic answer to a corporate problem. Societal structures—including those that offer access to education, housing, health, public facilities, and employment opportunities—have long facilitated white privilege. Despite the good work of well-meaning white evangelicals who love nonwhite people in their hearts, full progress toward racial justice will not be possible if societal structures are not critically addressed as well.

In 2020, the Council of Seminary Presidents of the Southern

Baptist Convention condemned "racism in any form" but also declared that "any version of Critical Theory is incompatible with the Baptist Faith and Message." Critical theory, often called critical race theory or CRT, asserts that racism and racial inequality result from social and institutional dynamics rather than individual prejudice. It holds that existing societal structures are biased toward the interests of white people and against marginalized communities. According to J. D. Greear, then president of the Southern Baptist Convention, "The Gospel gives a better answer" to problems of racism than does critical race theory.[25] Greear likely means that the gospel has the power to change human hearts and therefore enables people to turn away from their racist prejudices. This suggests that the gospel is a more powerful solution to racism than critical theories about systemic racism. But this response posits an either-or approach and may be overly simplistic, as pastor Timothy Keller suggests in his writing on justice.[26] Do evangelicals need to view critical race theory as an alternative to the gospel? Are Christians faced with a binary choice—either critical race theory or the gospel? That's like saying that the gospel is a better answer to the problem of murder than the law. On the one hand, of course it is! If the good news of God's love in Jesus Christ so transforms human hearts that people choose to love their enemies rather than murder them, that will be much more powerful than the law that simply forbids murder and punishes those who break it. But Christians do not therefore argue against laws prohibiting murder, since the gospel gives a better answer. The two are not mutually exclusive. We might prefer the gospel to do its work in every human heart so that there are no more murderers, but while we hold our breath for that, we should be glad that laws prohibit murder.

Black pastor Voddie Baucham's "war" on critical race theory is even less compelling. In his book *Fault Lines: The Social Justice Movement and Evangelicalism's Looming Catastrophe*, Baucham argues that because critical race theory is derived from a secular worldview rather than the Bible, it should be repudiated with all the spiritual weaponry Christians can muster.[27] But Christians embrace many concepts that are not directly derived from a biblical worldview. I wonder if Baucham also repudiates democracy and capitalism, both of which have little biblical support. Instead of knee-jerk reactions against "unbiblical" ideas and tools, Christians are wise to "plunder the Egyptians" when secular society develops useful tools. We don't have to buy into the worldview out of which they come any more than soccer moms become Hindu when they do yoga in the gym.

Critical race theory has its weaknesses—as any critical theory does—and its scholarly proponents differ on various points, but it may nevertheless serve as a useful tool in the fight against systemic racism. Perhaps the apparent incompatibility of evangelicalism and critical race theory has more to do with CRT's focus on corporate sin. By and large, evangelicals are overwhelmingly individualistic in their articulation and application of the gospel, eager to apply its message of personal salvation to individuals who repent of their own sins. But the interests of the Bible go farther than our individual sin and salvation. The Bible also recognizes societal structures that are built in defiance of the divine principles of love and equality. Such structures are critiqued and undermined by the message of Christ crucified. So the gospel of Jesus is not only about the transformation of individual human hearts but has wide-ranging implications for the whole of society, including its corrupt and prejudiced systems and institutions.

JESUS AND OUTSIDERS

What, then, is the answer to the "us versus them" mentality that drives evangelicals' exclusivity, seeing those who oppose them as enemies? It sounds like a cliché to suggest that the answer is love, but the answer *is* love. As Jonathan Pennington writes, "Love is . . . the great message and vision of Christianity."[28] But what sort of love are we talking about? Evangelicals know that biblically defined love is not mushy feelings, superficial niceties, or hollow acceptance. Scot McKnight describes biblically defined love as rugged commitment to be with and for others. Love is rugged commitment because it is often hard work. It is "with" because love is about sharing presence together. It is "for" because love means you will be their advocate, on their side.[29] It goes well beyond acceptance and affirmation, though it is not less than these. Jesus taught and modeled self-sacrificial commitment to the holistic welfare of others, along with genuine affection and intimate relationship. It is not enough to claim to love others while neglecting their welfare.

Loving Your Neighbor

Google "Good Samaritan stories" and you'll find several heart-warming accounts of unknown people coming to the rescue of strangers. Some of those stories are amazing and some are quite moving. But they all celebrate the kindness of a stranger. But what if I told you that the kindness of a stranger is not the main point of Jesus' famous parable of the good Samaritan? What if I told you that its main point is even more precious and important than that?

In Luke 10:25, an expert in the law of Moses gives Jesus a

pop quiz on how to inherit eternal life. Jesus answers the question with a question regarding the theologian's area of expertise: What does the law say? (v. 26). He answers correctly that one must love God and love their neighbor (v. 27). And while that might have been the end of the discussion, the theologian then asks a lawyer's question: "And who is my neighbor?" (v. 29). He seems to be looking for a legal loophole—if someone doesn't qualify as a neighbor, then we don't need to worry about loving them, right? Jesus challenges that subtext with the following parable.

A man traveling from Jerusalem to Jericho is mugged by bandits. He is stripped, beaten, and left for dead (v. 30). The beaten man is clearly a Jew—given his travel plans and Jesus' audience—but two religious Jews (a priest and a Levite) walk by without helping him (vv. 31–32).[30] At this point, the theologian may be thinking that Jesus is critiquing religious leaders like himself, and he probably expected a regular Jewish person to be the hero of the story. But no one listening to Jesus could have predicted what happens next. A Samaritan comes to the rescue of the beaten Jewish man and is the hero of the story (v. 33). That would have been totally surprising to Jesus' audience because the Jews and Samaritans were bitter rivals. Their mutual animosity was a type of sibling rivalry with a long history.[31] Indeed, Jesus' Jewish listeners, identifying with the man in the ditch, might have thought, "That Samaritan coming near is going to kill me."[32] So this is not just a "kindness of a stranger" story. The good Samaritan shows kindness to his enemy.

Why does the Samaritan show such kindness? We are simply told that when he saw the man, "he had compassion" (CSB). But he did not simply feel compassion for the beaten man. He acted.

He helped the man and took him to an inn where he could take good care of him (v. 34). The next day he paid the innkeeper to look after the Jewish man until his return (v. 35). Talk about kindness to a stranger! The Samaritan went above and beyond for this Jewish man in need—his bitter rival—spending his time and money to make sure he would be okay.

Jesus then wryly asks his theologian friend which of the three proved to be a neighbor to the befallen man (v. 36). Of course, it was the Samaritan—"The one who had mercy on him" (v. 37). If a Samaritan could be a good neighbor to the Jew, then the command to love your neighbor does not seem to have any limit. So Timothy Keller comments, "By depicting a Samaritan helping a Jew, Jesus could not have found a more forceful way to say that anyone at all in need—regardless of race, politics, class, and religion—is your neighbor."[33] It's not just the person living next door or some member of your community. It includes people from other countries and other ethnicities. It even includes your enemies (Matthew 5:44). Real love transcends all such boundaries. Love for our neighbor reaches across ethnic lines and extends to those who are different from us. It reaches those who may despise us or mistreat us.

To put a sharper edge on it, imagine this scenario. It's a rowdy night during one of the many Black Lives Matter protests of 2020 following the murder of George Floyd. A white Christian police officer is on edge, worried about his safety while trying to protect public property. He's been pushing up against protestors, showing some aggression but trying not to make things worse. Then some violent troublemakers overpower the police officer, separate him from his colleagues, and bash him. He finds himself lying in an alley alone, bleeding and semiconscious. Who will come to his aid? Some white university students spot him but rush by. A white pastor and his wife hurry past, wanting to avoid any hint of violence. And a group of protestors spots him but moves on with the crowd. In the end, a gay Black BLM advocate comes to his rescue. He checks the police officer's injuries and calls an ambulance. He tends to his wounds and assures him that help is on the way. He guides the ambulance to the alley and makes sure the officer is in good hands. The next day, the Good Samaritan visits the police officer in hospital and brings him a get-well basket with fresh fruit, cheeses, chocolate, and some wine (for later).

Is that story hard to believe?

In a world torn apart by deep-seated divisions—ethnic, racial, economic, sexual, and political—we all need to hear the message of Jesus' parable of the good Samaritan. He says "go and do likewise" (Luke 10:37 NIV). So how will Jesus' followers do that? Whom do evangelicals consider their neighbor? How will they treat people who are different from them? If Jesus' followers share God's heart, they too will show compassion to those in need no matter who they are.

Loving Your Enemy

If the parable of the good Samaritan is designed to challenge our sense of who our neighbor is, Jesus' Sermon on the Mount blows right past that question. "You have heard that it was said, 'Love your neighbor and hate your enemy.' But I tell you, love your enemies and pray for those who persecute you, that you may be children of your Father in heaven. He causes his sun to rise on the evil and the good, and sends rain on the righteous and the unrighteous. If you love those who love you, what reward will you get? Are not even the tax collectors doing that? And if you greet only your own people, what are you doing more than others? Do not even pagans do that?" (Matthew 5:43–47).

Jesus takes loving your neighbor to the next level and tells his followers to love their enemies and pray for them. For people oppressed under the cultural and financial boot of the Roman Empire, "hating one's enemies seemed not only natural but divinely patriotic," says Jonathan Pennington, just like "a modern notion of 'Christian' America that is interpreted as standing up against certain aspects of culture and government."[34] But by loving their enemies, Jesus' followers will show themselves to be children of God, who gives good things to all. While everyone knows how to take care of their loved ones, his followers need to show love beyond their own. If they do that, they will be like their Father in heaven.

It is clear that evangelicals do have enemies, a fact that can make them a bit paranoid. But, as they say, just because you're paranoid doesn't mean they're not out to get you. Some people clearly are out to get evangelicals. They might attack, harass, or persecute without much provocation. Some of that enmity comes to evangelicals because the movement is regarded as homophobic, racist, or xenophobic. But what will Jesus' followers do in response to such enmity? Following Jesus on this is really hard, but his point about being children of God demonstrates that the key is who you are. Following Jesus is not just about doing this or that, it is about *being* a certain kind of person, and none of us starts out as that kind of person. We may become that way only through the transformation of the heart as we are shaped by God's compassion for his wayward creatures. He sees our need and comes to our rescue even though we have turned against him

(Romans 5:8, 10). All good evangelicals know this and believe it, so why is it so hard for them to apply it to their enemies? Could it be that God's love in Christ has yet to change their hearts so that they might show the same love to others?

While some people are out to get evangelicals, most are not. Evangelicals might consider people their enemies because of a different worldview, their sexuality, or their political preferences, even if these individuals are not trying to oppose them. Evangelicals must not assume "the other" is the enemy. Instead, they should think of the other as *another*—another neighbor. And as we've seen, followers of Jesus are to show love to their neighbors whoever they may be. Scot McKnight comments, "When the church is the church it is fully engaged in loving everyone as neighbors."[35] My longtime friend Dave Steel once said, "It's hard to demonize someone when you get to know them." I have seen the truth of that observation countless times. Without personal knowledge of someone, it is far too easy to make assumptions about them based on their appearance, ethnicity, sexuality, or economic status. Time and again I have been surprised by how wrong my assumptions were once I engaged a person in conversation and got to know them a little. If we want to treat "the other" as our neighbor rather than our enemy, we should start there.

Love also boldly decides to confess corporate sin. Jemar Tisby tells the story of Second Presbyterian Church in Memphis, Tennessee, a church that had once refused to admit Black members. Half a century later, church leaders formed a committee to address the church's racist past and made four recommendations: "(1) reveal to the congregation the racist origins of the church, and adopt the denominational stance on race and the gospel, (2) study what the Bible said about individual and corporate repentance, (3) publicly confess and repent of racism, and (4) recommit to serving their local community across racial and ethnic lines."[36]

If evangelicals want to be known for their love of all people, it may be necessary first to make some corporate confessions of their failures to do so.

Love refuses to make enemies of those opposed to us. But love goes even farther, seeking the good of others ahead of our own. According to Dallas Willard and Gary Black Jr., "In the larger social, governmental, or economic setting, those motivated by love do what they can to establish and sustain arrangements and practices that will benefit everyone or as many as possible."[37] How many evangelicals stop to consider whether loving their neighbor might sometimes mean voting against their own interests? Will white evangelicals vote against their own interests for the sake of racial equality, even if it might decrease their privileges? How many evangelicals would be willing to walk into a gay bar to befriend some *people* (who happen to be gay)? Perhaps the discomfort they'd experience would give them some insight into what it's like for an outsider to walk into their churches.

THREE

BAD JUDGMENT

Do not judge, or you too will be judged.

ROSARIA BUTTERFIELD WAS A LEFTIST PROFESSOR OF LITERA-
ture at Syracuse University. As a feminist and lesbian, she was
speechless when in 1997 the Christian group Promise Keepers
held a two-day event at the university. She criticized the university's decision to allow the group to use the campus for a
weekend, and she wrote an article in the local newspaper attack-
ing Promise Keepers.

She received quite a lot of hate mail in response to her
article, but one letter stood out. It was from the pastor of the
Syracuse Reformed Presbyterian Church, Ken Smith. The letter
was respectful and kind, but probing as Smith asked Butterfield
to defend her presuppositions. The letter bothered Butterfield
and caused her to consider the validity of her historical mate-
rialist worldview. The letter also initiated her friendship with
Ken and his wife, Floy. Her previous experience of Christians

included those "who mocked me on Gay Pride Day," but that was not what Ken did: "He did not mock. He engaged." Ken and Floy "entered my world. They met my friends. We did book exchanges. We talked openly about sexuality and politics."

Rosaria began to read the Bible, reading it several times over the course of a year. She fought against it with all her might, but it overflowed into her world. One day on her own accord, she "rose from the bed of [her] lesbian lover, and an hour later sat in a pew at the Syracuse Reformed Presbyterian Church. . . .

"Then, one ordinary day, I came to Jesus, openhanded and naked. In this war of worldviews, Ken was there. Floy was there. The church that had been praying for me for years was there. Jesus triumphed."[1]

The beautiful story of Rosaria's unlikely conversion demonstrates how important it is to show grace and charity toward those outside the church. It all began with Ken's gracious letter in response to Rosaria's newspaper article. The tone of that letter, along with the warm friendship that followed, were the factors that God used to bring Rosaria to faith in Christ. However, Ken's letter was the exception. It stood out among the many hostile attacks that Rosaria endured from other Christians.

PERCEPTION AND REALITY

Evangelicalism suffers from the perception and reality of judgmentalism. One of America's leading polling organizations, the Barna Group, surveyed non-Christians ages sixteen to twenty-nine in 2007 and found that 87 percent of respondents viewed Christianity as judgmental.[2] Barna has tracked this perception since then, and not much has changed. Recently a number of high-profile pastors have reinforced the perception of evangelical judgmentalism by claiming that the coronavirus pandemic is God's judgment on a sinful America.[3]

The judgmental evangelical is a well-worn trope in Hollywood, literature, and pop culture. But are the media and mainstream culture being fair to evangelicals in this regard? I used to think they were very unfair. They don't know me and my friends, I thought. They don't know my church and the many fine Christians there and elsewhere. And most evangelicals are like us, not like the stereotypes perpetuated "out there." It's all just part of an ungodly conspiracy to paint Christians in the worst possible light. That's what I used to think. Now I'm not so sure. To begin, there are actual examples of evangelical judgmentalism to be observed in the public square, such as the suggestion that anyone who votes Democrat is not a real Christian. But should these examples be dismissed as the crazy few who give the others a bad name? Does the problem go deeper than that?

The sharpest judgmentalism I've experienced was from evangelicals in the wake of my failed marriage. I will talk more about that in a later chapter, but for now I will say that those experiences helped me to better understand the perception of evangelicals as judgmental. I realized this experience was more than just perception. It was real.

Evangelical judgmentalism is aimed at both unbelievers and nonconforming believers. For some evangelicals, divorce is one of those unacceptable sins that permits the defamation, alienation, and abuse of offenders. And there are several other unacceptable sins too, like homosexual practice, gender dysphoria, and voting Democrat. These unacceptable sins permit judgment.

Self-righteousness is one factor that fuels evangelical judgmentalism. The self-righteous person might not think that they're perfect, but they set standards of behavior and morality for themselves that they easily meet. It's a little like creating an exam for yourself, which, of course, you're able to pass. But others might not pass, so the self-righteous person feels justified in judging them. The self-righteous person says, "I know I'm not perfect, but at least I don't . . ." or, "I've made mistakes, but I'm not as bad as that divorced guy." Evangelicals know themselves to be sinners, since the gospel tells them so. No evangelical will claim to be perfect or without sin. But they will nevertheless hold to sets of acceptable and unacceptable sins. And anyone who commits an unacceptable sin will likely fall victim to evangelical scorn and repudiation.

The root of our self-righteousness is a lack of humility. Sure, many evangelicals will think they're humble (if it's possible to think that without losing your humility). But humility is relative. Some might believe they were blind without God's light, but they remain stubborn about their views and practices. Others might demonstrate humility before God, knowing they need his mercy and forgiveness, but will be arrogant and judgmental toward others who also need that grace. Some evangelicals might look down on those who don't belong to their tribe, while others might condemn them as God haters and apostates. Evangelicals will sometimes denounce any who disagree with their claims to the truth.

Counterintuitively, a lack of humility can be a sign of insecurity—another element that fuels judgmentalism. Judgmental people derive satisfaction from looking down on others because it props up their sense of superiority. Insecurity is

61

a powerful driver of criticism, slander, jealousy, and judgment. Insecure people find it hard to affirm others, often interpreting such affirmation as a loss of power. But they can be quick to pounce on errors, weaknesses, and differences, as though doing so increases their own stock. In reality, they're just being jerks.

JESUS V. JUDGMENT

My theological analysis—more reliable than my armchair psychologizing—suggests that judgmentalism stems from being out of step with the heart of God. Knowing the heart of God diffuses self-righteousness, inspires humility, and offers lasting security. And the heart of God longs to extend love, mercy, and forgiveness to all.

Contrary to the impression that evangelical culture makes, Christianity is opposed to judging others. And that's because Jesus was opposed to it. He strongly instructed his followers to resist judging others, and he demonstrated the opposite of judgmentalism in his interactions with people. He regularly butted heads with religious leaders who presumed to make judgments about other people, condemning *their* condemnation of others.

Do Not Judge

In Matthew 7:1, Jesus says, "Do not judge, or you too will be judged." Simple words. Do not judge. To be sure, there is a place for some kinds of judgment, but according to biblical scholar Grant Osborne, the type of judgment that Jesus forbids here is the kind we've been discussing: the act of "looking down on a person with a superior attitude, criticizing or condemning them without a loving concern."[4] Evangelicals today have developed a reputation for this kind of judgment, to the point where evangelicals are expected to be judgmental. Long before the Trump era, evangelicals in Western culture suffered a negative image as being judgmental people.

Matthew 7:1 is more than a command, it is also a prediction. "Do not judge, *or you too will be judged.*" Some understand this to refer to God's eschatological judgment, inferring that judgmentalism is one of the many sins for which people will need to answer to God one day. But more likely, Jesus is referring to the response to our judgment—the judgment of others toward those who judge them. Biblical scholar Jonathan Pennington comments, "If one has a condemning attitude toward others, this will be one's experience of the world."[5] And that seems to be what evangelicals are experiencing today. They are regarded as bad people *because* they judge others. Judging others remains one of the few things still regarded as immoral in Western culture. The only exception to this rule is that it is okay to judge judgmental people. And so evangelicals routinely experience the second half of Matthew 7:1—they are judged by a society that will no longer tolerate their judgment.

Jesus goes on to explain that you will be judged by the measure you use to judge others (v. 2) and that you need to move the plank out of your own eye before you can remove the speck of sawdust from your brother's eye (vv. 3–5). This doesn't mean that once you remove the plank from your own eye you are allowed to judge others. The key to understanding this instruction is Jesus' statement in verse 5: "then you will see clearly to remove the speck from your brother's eye." The issue is gaining the ability to see clearly.[6]

I think there are two reasons why Jesus forbids us to judge others. First, we are not God, who is the rightful judge of all (Romans 12:19). And second, unlike God, we do not see clearly enough to judge rightly. Our vision is corrupted by our prejudices, preferences, personalities, and distinct lack of omniscience. Any judgment we make will always be based on partial information. And that information might be flawed. Though the Bible regularly exhorts believers to be imitators of God (Ephesians 5:1), judgment is an activity we are not to imitate. That it is something we are not to imitate underscores the extent to which judgment belongs to God alone. It is too hot to handle. We will mess it up. And the well-being of others hangs in the balance. God does not trust us to judge, and rightly so.

Or You Too Will Be Judged

On one occasion, Jesus accepted an invitation to eat at a Pharisee's home, and a woman who is described only as "a sinner" invited herself along to be with Jesus (Luke 7:36–37, 39). In an extraordinary display of affection, the woman washed Jesus' feet with her tears, wiped them with her hair, kissed them, and anointed them with expensive perfume (v. 38). Imagine the scene. Most people would be moved by such a display of affection. We don't know what the woman did to deserve the description "a sinner," but Luke's readers probably imagined her an adulteress or a prostitute.[7] Regardless of what she had done, she was a woman in anguish, and she humbled herself before Jesus in her sorrow.

But Jesus' host, Simon, did not see a beautiful display of affection and sorrow. He saw evidence that Jesus was not a prophet, since he apparently did not know what kind of woman was touching him—a sinner (v. 39). Notice his assumption that Jesus would not have associated with her if he had known who she was. He believed that a righteous man like Jesus would want nothing to do with a sinner like her. But Jesus' powers of perception focused on his host, rather than on the sinful woman, and he decided to say something to Simon (v. 40). He shared a miniparable about two debtors. Jesus spoke of two people in debt to a lender—one owing five hundred denarii (about one and three-quarters years' wages), and the other one-tenth of that amount (about two months' wages) (v. 41).[8] Neither one could repay their debt, so the lender forgave them both. Then Jesus asked, "Which of them will love him more?" (v. 42). Simon answered correctly—the one forgiven more would love more (v. 43). But then Jesus flipped the narrative, contrasting Simon's treatment of him with the woman's. He pointed out how Simon had shown little hospitality to Jesus, but the woman had treated him like a king (vv. 44–46). Since her many sins had been forgiven, she loved much. But someone forgiven little loves little (v. 47). Jesus then released the woman from her sins (v. 48).

How does this story address judgmentalism? First, both debtors in the parable were in trouble. Neither could pay their debt. Just because one debt was ten times more than the other does not mean the smaller debt was not a problem. Both debtors needed and received forgiveness, an indication of God's gracious willingness to forgive all who need it, regardless of how much forgiveness is needed. Second, it highlights how God's forgiveness is received. Simon the Pharisee thought he was not a great sinner, so his welcome of Jesus was lukewarm. He did not think he had great need for God's grace, so his love was weak. But the woman knew her failures. She knew she needed forgiveness. She knew she needed Jesus. So she welcomed him with her whole heart, responding with heartfelt love and gratitude. Third, the story demonstrates exactly what Jesus warns about in Matthew 7:1—"Do not judge, or you too will be judged." Simon the Pharisee judged the woman because she was sinful, and he even judged Jesus for associating with her. But Jesus forgave the woman's sins rather than judge her. He did, however, judge Simon, because Simon had wrongly judged them.

Evangelicals who claim to be forgiven of their sin yet deep down believe they are more moral, more respectful of God, and more pleasing to him than others will tend to think they have less need of God's grace. And as a result, they might actually love God less and prove Jesus' point here. But those who know their need of forgiveness and receive forgiveness will love much. The danger of judging others is that we are able neither to see others' hearts nor to know whether God has forgiven them. The irony of judging others without knowledge of God's judgment is that we unwittingly bring judgment upon ourselves. Instead of reflecting Jesus' love and compassion, evangelicals who are prone to judgment are more like Jesus' self-righteous religious opponents.

Judgment v. Discernment

In 1 Corinthians, Paul rebukes the Corinthians for celebrating a situation in which a man has apparently been sleeping with his stepmother (5:1–2). Paul instructs that this man is to be put out of the fellowship until he is restored, so that he will be spared God's judgment (vv. 4–5). He then speaks about those who claim to be Christians but really are not, as seen by their behavior (vv. 9–11). Paul concludes that God will judge those outside the church, but Christians are to judge those inside it and expel the wicked person from among them (vv. 12–13). This passage seems to contradict Jesus' instruction in Matthew 7:1 not to judge. While believers should not judge those outside the church, Paul seems to say that insiders are fair game.

But in context, it is clear that Paul is addressing church discipline, which Jesus also addresses in Matthew 18:15–17. In that passage, Jesus encourages his followers to approach—in a gentle and private manner—the brother or sister who has sinned. If they listen, the matter is over (v. 15). Then Jesus addresses what should be done if they do not listen, which can escalate all the way to deciding to treat them like an unbeliever (vv. 16–17). Jesus' teachings in Matthew 7:1 ("do not judge") and Matthew 18:15–17 ("point out their fault") therefore do not contradict each other. What he calls judgment in Matthew 7:1 is a proud condemnation of another person. It is looking down on someone from a position of moral superiority. But the picture in Matthew 18:15–17 is very different. It's clear that the well-being of the other person is of paramount importance. There is no hint of moral superiority or of looking down on someone. The desire is not to condemn, it is to restore.[9] Paul's instructions in 1 Corinthians 5 are likewise concerned with restoration, not condemnation.[10] In this way, he parallels Jesus in Matthew 18:15–17 and does not contradict him in Matthew 7:1.

This is an example of how the word *judge* can mean different things depending on the context. If I say, "Don't judge me," you would understand that to mean something like, "Don't sit in judgment over me; don't condemn me." But if I say, "I think she is a good judge of character," you would understand that to mean something like, "She is discerning about people's character." In the Greek, both senses are carried by one word, much like our word *judge* in English.[11] Jesus says don't judge, condemn, or look down on someone else. But he also encourages his followers to show discernment that will help them to restore someone stuck in sin. The latter is what Paul means when he says that believers are to judge those inside the church. They are to discern in order to restore.

The Motivation Is Always Love

Contrary to the "don't judge me" type of judgment, Christian discernment is always to be motivated by love. If we spot someone engaged in a destructive mindset or behavior, helping them to overcome it is an act of love. Jesus shows that such motivation must also be matched by the tone of approach, which is to be gentle and private. It is not rash or harsh. It is not an excuse for gossip or group condemnation. On the contrary, sitting in judgment over someone or looking down on them from a position of moral superiority is the opposite of love. There is no concern for the other person, no interest in their restoration. There is only self-righteous pride and unholy indignation.

THE HEART OF GOD

At the heart of judgmentalism is a failure to know the heart of God. Who God is, and how his heart beats for us, is the key to loving rather than judging others. Two more of Jesus' parables recounted by Luke reveal the nature of God's heart, and I can think of no better way to make my point than simply to retell these stories.

The Father's Compassion

The parable of the prodigal son says much about God's heart. In Luke 15, Jesus speaks to the "tax collectors and sinners" who have gathered to listen to him, and to the religious leaders who complain that Jesus welcomes such people (vv. 1–2). The parable corrects the attitude that God would associate only with "good" people. Instead, we see that God's heart is full of compassion and that as Father, he welcomes those who draw near to him. The twist is that those who do not welcome "tax collectors and sinners" are the ones who are out of step with God.[12]

In the parable, when the young son asks his father for his share of the estate (v. 12), he effectively says, "I wish you were already dead, but since you aren't, I can't wait any longer," as biblical scholar David Garland puts it.[13] This would have been deeply offensive to the father, but he grants his son's wish without comment (v. 12b). Then we see the son's intent: he takes off to a distant place, where no one knows him, so he can spend his father's money indulging his every desire without fear of accountability (v. 13). But his anonymity becomes a double-edged sword, since no one cares when he runs out of money and begins to be in need. He gets a job, but it pays so badly that the pigs he feeds are better off than he is (vv. 14–16). His unjust boss causes him to realize that his father is a good man who pays his employees generously (v. 17). So the son decides to return to his father. He recognizes his sin and that he has effectively given up his sonship. He will request only to be one of his father's employees (vv. 18–19).

As the son approaches home, the father spots him at a distance (v. 20). Has the father been watching for his return? Has he been keeping an eye on the horizon in hope? And before the son can say anything, his father is filled with compassion and runs and embraces his son (v. 20). Even though dignified West Asian men do not run, this father does not care about custom.[14] He makes himself look foolish as he hitches up his robe and runs without thought of his appearance. He sees the object of his love and rushes to embrace him. When the son gives his prepared speech, the father responds by treating his son like a prince and throwing him a big party (vv. 21–24).

The father's older son responds negatively to this. He hears the party, but instead of going in and asking his father what is going on, he stays outside and asks one of the servants, who explains what the fuss is about (vv. 25–27). The son becomes angry and pouts (v. 28). But notice what the father does. He leaves the party and pleads with him to join in. But the older son is rude to him. He complains that he has been "slaving" for his father all these years, yet never once celebrated with his friends. He complains about his brother's immorality and objects that he should be celebrated (vv. 28–30). It seems this son does not really regard himself as part of the family. He is a slave of his father, rather than a son. He calls his brother "this son of yours" rather than his own brother. He talks about celebrating with friends rather than with his family. While the younger son realizes he no longer has a right to be his father's son, the older son does not treat him as a father either. But the father does not chide his older son for being so petty and callous. He calls him son. He affirms their relationship and that he shares everything with him. But he also gently corrects this son, reminding him that his brother is his brother and that it's right to celebrate his return (vv. 31–32).

The point of the story is to show God's fatherly heart.[15] He is Father to the wayward son, and Father to the obedient but relationally distant son. God loves both. And he wants the older son to share his heart for the wayward son. As Jesus speaks to the religious leaders, he encourages them first to know God's heart, and second to adopt the same attitude in their hearts. They should welcome tax collectors and sinners too, as Jesus did. Some readers may identify with the wayward son, and others may identify with the obedient but distant son. Either way, all need to know God's heart. He loves all. He wants us to know him as Father. And he wants us to share his heart for the lost, the wayward, and the rebellious. If we know God's heart and share his heart, there will be no room for judgmentalism in our hearts.

God Hates Pride but Lifts Up the Humble

In the parable of the Pharisee and the tax collector, Jesus takes aim at "some who trusted in themselves . . . and looked down on everyone else" (Luke 18:9 CSB). Jesus tells of two men going to the temple to pray—a common image, as people regularly went to the temple for daily worship services.[16] But the story gets interesting when we're told that one of the men is a Pharisee—a moral and upright religious figure—and the other a tax collector—someone despised by Jews because he collects taxes to pay the Romans (their oppressors). Tax collectors were known to regularly rip off their own people too. The Pharisee and the tax collector are opposites, and Jesus' listeners would picture them as the good guy (Pharisee) and the bad guy (tax collector). That's what makes the conclusion of this story highly unexpected: in the end the tax collector is right with God and the Pharisee is not (v. 14).

Why is this so? First, remember that the scene is likely a

public temple gathering. The prayers offered by the two men are not private silent prayers (like in an empty church on a weekday, as is often depicted in movies).[17] The Pharisee stands and thanks God out loud that he is not like other bad people, including the tax collector, who can no doubt hear the Pharisee's prayer (v. 11). Then he boasts of his good deeds (v. 12). Just imagine someone standing at the front of church today and thanking God that they are better than everyone else there. That's the picture Jesus paints. And notice what the Pharisee does not pray about. He does not ask God for anything. He does not ask for forgiveness. There is no humility and no expression of dependence on God. And there is no recognition of who God is.

Now consider the tax collector's prayer. He stands far off and can't look to heaven, since he is ashamed of himself. He repeatedly pounds his chest, which in that culture is an expression of extreme anguish and is normally done only by women. His prayer is simple: "God, have mercy on me, a sinner" (v. 13). He acknowledges his sin and failure. He acknowledges he needs God's mercy. And he implicitly acknowledges that God is merciful. His prayer "have mercy" literally means "turn your wrath away from me," which asks God to direct his just judgment away from him even though he deserves it.[18]

When Jesus declares that the tax collector "went home justified" (v. 14a), he teaches that the one who humbles himself, acknowledges his failures, and depends on God's kindness rather than his own status will be right with God. On the contrary, someone who is proud, self-reliant, and confident of his own impressiveness will not be right with God. Such a person is simply incorrect about himself and about God. No one is actually self-reliant; we are all wholly dependent on God's good gifts.

No one knocks God out with their impressiveness. The Pharisee thinks that God views people as being in competition for his approval, which is simply untrue.

The heart of the matter is that "all those who exalt themselves will be humbled, and those who humble themselves will be exalted" (v. 14b). God hates pride. God lifts up the humble (Proverbs 3:34). God's values are not the values of this world, which often prizes strength over weakness, pride over humility, and self-reliance over dependence. Those who humble themselves recognize who they really are and who God really is. There are many humble evangelicals. But there are also many who desperately need to hear Jesus' message. Pride, impressiveness, and looking down on others are not pleasing to God. These are the very things that will cause God to judge proud evangelicals. The self-confessed sinner—the one looked down on by judgmental people—is the one justified by God, rather than the self-righteous proud religious figure.

As I've been writing this chapter, I've reflected on my complicity in judging others and I've reflected on those who've stood over me in judgment. For the former, I've needed forgiveness. Regarding the latter, as the target of judgment, I've experienced hurt, confusion, and anger. But the Lord has given me peace. I offer them forgiveness in the name of Jesus.

FOUR

TRIBALISM

*By this everyone will know that you are
my disciples, if you love one another.*

RUDYARD KIPLING'S POEM "WE AND THEY" OFFERS AN INSIGHTful exploration of tribalism. The final stanza reads:

> All good people agree,
> And all good people say,
> All nice people, like Us, are We
> And every one else is They:
> But if you cross over the sea,
> Instead of over the way,
> You may end by (think of it!) looking on We
> As only a sort of They!

Divisiveness is one of the great sins in the Bible. And evangelicals have a history of exacerbating their differences rather

74

than bonding over the core tenets of their shared faith. Such dividing lines tend to be set according to tribal values rather than biblical teaching. Approved theology regarding central issues is determined by the tribe or its key leaders. And what constitutes a central issue is determined by the tribe too. For instance, a different interpretation of a single verse from Revelation (20:4) was regarded important enough to divide evangelicals into different tribes a century ago. When I joined the faculty of Trinity Evangelical Divinity School, its statement of faith (adopted from the Evangelical Free Church of America) still included the eschatological position of premillennialism, which each faculty member had to affirm. Thankfully that vestige of yesteryear's tribalism has been expunged from the EFCA's statement of faith.

Some might object to my analysis of how approved theology is derived. They would argue that evangelical theology is shaped by the Bible, because evangelicals are Bible people. Biblicism is one of the key distinctives of evangelicalism, as we will explore. But the issue is rather more complex than that, since the Bible may be read in several different ways. Unsurprisingly, evangelical theology derives from an evangelical way of reading the Bible that favors texts that support evangelical theology. The result is an interpretive grid through which the Bible is read. And this grid is particularly difficult to critique because if the grid is derived from the Bible, it means that evangelical theology must be biblical. The truth is that any type of interpretive grid for reading the Bible—whether it be evangelical, liberal Protestant, or Catholic—will inevitably distort the message of the whole Bible by privileging certain texts and themes while marginalizing or ignoring others. As David Gushee comments, "The Bible is always an interpreted text, and . . . we flawed, limited, self-interested people are the interpreters."[1]

CHURCH FAULT LINES

Not all divisions are bad. Some are even necessary. Within evangelicalism there are formal organizational divisions, such as denominations, and informal theological divisions, such as Calvinism and Arminianism. There are also divisions based on philosophies of ministry, such as megachurches and home churches. Organizational divisions are often motivated by theological differences (at least initially), just as philosophies of ministry are affected by theology. It is an unfortunate but inevitable outcome of Protestant freethinking that this wing of Christianity has fragmented into a thousand pieces, while Catholicism and Eastern Orthodoxy remain more or less monolithic (at least organizationally). While many evangelicals might prefer greater unity, the long history of splitting over differences often means that working together is difficult or impossible. Separate organizational structures eventually become necessary, but organizational divisions (such as denominations) do not necessitate divided fellowship. Denominations will sometimes work together for shared causes, and churches of different stripes often engage in friendly relations with one another. Evangelicals can be good at cross-denominational partnership, with shared evangelical convictions sometimes offering stronger bonds than they might enjoy within their own denominations. In Australia, many evangelical Anglicans feel they have more in common with evangelical Presbyterians and Baptists than with nonevangelical

Anglicans. Their shared evangelicalism is stronger than their denominational ties.

Less acceptable forms of division run along cultural lines. Though Christ commissioned his disciples to make disciples of all nations, and Revelation pictures the gathered church as a multifaceted, multiracial, and multicultural entity, churches are often monochromatic. While Black churches and white churches have formed according to the segregation inherent in many American cities, and other culturally specific churches (such as Asian) form because of language differences or a particular mission focus, too many Christians choose a church simply because they want to be with people who are like them. In their hearts, many believers do not fully embrace the barrier-destroying nature of Christ's ministry, despite the proclamation of the gospel from evangelical pulpits.

Another type of division is political. It is abhorrent to see Jesus' church aligned to a political party, whether Republican or Democrat. As we discussed in the first chapter, there is a difference between being political and being partisan. A church in the pocket of a particular party is not able to be a prophetic witness to truth, justice, and peace in the political sphere. How can it critique a party's unrighteous elements if the church has no other political option and the party knows it? The agenda of the church and the agenda of its party will merge into one, creating an unholy mix of worldly and otherworldly priorities. Aware of this dynamic, but feeling powerless in the face of prevailing political assumptions, some faithful church members are too afraid to talk about politics at all. They don't feel safe telling others they voted Democrat, and they quietly leave their Republican-aligned fellowship, while those who hold more conservative political views might not feel they have a safe place to share those views in a church that aligns itself with Democratic political positions.

A final form of division occurs when some churches unite around powerful personas or celebrity preachers. While they claim to gather in the name of Christ, the reality is that these individuals are the drawing card. Evangelicals love their celebrities. And while there's nothing wrong with wanting to hear a preacher who really blesses you, it's a problem when the celebrity preacher becomes a point of unity or division. In several instances, a celebrity preacher has come under criticism and the tribal response has been to rally around the tribal figure rather than to weigh the criticism appropriately.

Many factors splinter the evangelical world. Some are less destructive than others. But we can all agree that the degree of division in the evangelical church is greater than we would like, let alone what Jesus would like. And while we should be aware of the various reasons why division exists, the greatest cause of division is often theological, which reflects the importance of the Bible among evangelical churches. And it reflects different views about how the Bible is read.

TRIBAL READINGS

Since the Bible is their final authority in matters of faith, evangelicals should welcome biblical correction of evangelical theology. But this is often not the case because the evangelical grid of biblical interpretation is *de facto* the highest authority, rather than the Bible itself. Some texts are privileged over others, and texts that don't fit the grid tend to be marginalized or ignored.

As we saw in the introduction, historian David Bebbington's four priorities of evangelicalism, or his quadrilateral, are conversionism, activism, biblicism, and crucicentrism.[2] Conversionism is the belief that people must be converted to be right with God. Activism refers to the attitude that the gospel must be expressed through effort. Biblicism refers to a particular regard for the Bible as the highest authority in matters of faith. Crucicentrism refers to a focus on the atoning work of Christ through his death on the cross. Bebbington's quadrilateral summarizes a historical analysis of evangelicalism in modern Britain from the 1730s to 1980s and does not necessarily describe all of those who identify as evangelicals today. Indeed, British evangelicals differ significantly from American evangelicals, further underscoring how the term *evangelical* is losing or has lost much of its meaning. Many self-professed evangelicals no longer meet Bebbington's description of an evangelical. And the wider public, including the mainstream media, do not even understand or consider Bebbington's description of evangelicalism, using the term for different purposes. In America, an evangelical is typically understood to be a white Christian nationalist, a reality noted by Thomas Kidd and several others.[3] For a majority of Americans, conversionism, activism, biblicism, and crucicentrism have little to do with the definition of an evangelical.

Tribal Emphases

The problems with evangelicalism, however, go beyond the eroding meaning of that term. There are problems inherent to the quadrilateral itself, and the chief of these relates to the evangelical priority of biblicism. By upholding the authority of the Bible in matters of faith, evangelicals ought to be committed to the full extent of biblical teaching. But in reality evangelicals are selective in their theological emphases, particularly when the Bible is interpreted through another element of Bebbington's quadrilateral: crucicentrism. Evangelicals are correct to view Christ's death as central to the teaching of the Bible. But they will sometimes emphasize the cross at the expense of other central themes, such as Christ's resurrection. No good evangelical would pit the death of Christ against his resurrection, as though focusing on the resurrection is somehow not evangelical or less than evangelical. But in practice the reality is often so. Ask an evangelical what the gospel is, and ten out of ten answers will include the central significance of the cross. But fewer than ten answers will mention the resurrection. While the New Testament holds Jesus' death and resurrection together as centrally significant, evangelicals' emphasis is often lopsided, reflecting tribal emphases.

In Sydney Anglican circles in Australia, where I did my seminary training and my first seven years of New Testament lecturing, student preachers were regularly exhorted to "preach the cross" regardless of what biblical text was in view. Beloved late evangelist John Chapman instructed would-be preachers that if they did not include the cross in their sermons, they had not preached the gospel. I loved "Chappo" and learned much from him, but I sometimes felt uneasy about the degree of his crucicentrism. Students debated whether it is okay to preach any text from the Bible without talking about Jesus' death. The usual consensus was no. It was a given that Jesus should be preached (even if he was not mentioned in the text), but why could a preacher not focus on his resurrection instead of his cross? Or what about his ascension? Or what about his incarnation, baptism, transfiguration, teachings, or miracles? No, it should be the cross. But this was not the opinion of the apostles. According to the Acts of the Apostles, they regularly preached the resurrection of Jesus without explaining his atoning death.[4] On this point, I remember Chappo saying, "Well, if Jesus' resurrection is mentioned, it implies his death, so you get it in that way." But that misses the point. The point is that in the apostles' preaching, they sometimes did not focus on the cross at all, which raises the question as to why evangelicals insist on preaching the cross every time, even when it is not the focus of the passage. As a result, evangelical crucicentrism shuts down the interpretive options available to preachers when handling various biblical texts. Evangelicals want to talk about the cross even if it means playing down the text's emphasis. In that way, evangelical crucicentrism subtly undermines evangelical biblicism by not allowing the Bible to speak. The biblical meaning is flattened to a variation on a single theme, losing its diverse richness as it is simplified into the black-and-white message of "sin and the cross."

But evangelical crucicentrism is even more problematic than a flattening of biblical interpretation. Not only must the cross be preached but a particular interpretation of the cross must be preached. This interpretation is known as penal substitutionary atonement (PSA). PSA is the biblical teaching that in his death, Jesus paid the penalty for human sin. His death was penal because he paid a price for sin. It was substitutionary because he died in place of others. And it was an atonement because through his penal substitutionary death, Jesus enabled sinful human beings to be reconciled to God. I describe PSA as biblical because the New Testament does teach this meaning of the cross of Jesus (1 Peter 2:24). To be clear, I am not opposed to PSA. However, I want to make it equally clear that PSA is not the only significance of Jesus' death.

The so-called *Christus Victor* interpretation of the cross presents Jesus as conquering the forces of sin, death, and the devil through his death. It is about Jesus' victory over cosmic evil and his overthrow of the final enemy—death itself. This model of the atonement is also biblical. It is not at odds with PSA (though it is sometimes understood as such) but complements it.[5] Yet evangelicals rarely present Jesus' death this way. Jesus' death is also presented as an example for others to follow. Believers are to endure injustice just as Jesus did in his unjust crucifixion and, like Jesus, entrust themselves to the one who judges justly (1 Peter 2:21–23). To be sure, it would be a mistake to claim that the only significance of Jesus' death is the example he set (as is often argued by liberal Protestants). But it would also be a mistake to say that Jesus does not set an example through his cross. He does. And the Bible says so. Years ago a student brought to my attention that I had preached a "subjective atonement" because in a sermon I had drawn attention to Jesus' example in his death. By subjective atonement this student meant that Jesus' death was understood as affecting one's subjective attitude rather than objective status as forgiven for their sins and reconciled to God. The implication was that we don't preach a subjective atonement because that's liberal stuff. But it is not liberal stuff. The apostle Peter believed Jesus' death was an example for us to follow, and that's good enough for me even if it contravenes evangelical crucicentrism.

Because evangelical crucicentrism often focuses exclusively on penal substitutionary atonement and downplays or ignores other elements of Jesus' cross, sin is nearly always treated as personal and individualistic. Jesus died for *my* sins. Jesus took *my* place on the cross. Jesus paid the penalty *I* deserve for my sins. To be sure, the Bible does present sin as personal and individualistic. But it is far more varied than that. Sin is also portrayed as communal, systemic, and even cosmic. In Ephesians 2:1–3, Paul views human sin as part of a complex bigger picture in which unbelievers follow the ways of this world and "the ruler of the kingdom of the air," the spirit at work within them. It would not be sufficient, then, to say that Jesus died for my sins if he does not also rescue believers from their captivity to capital-*S* Sin, the ruler and master that keeps them as slaves (Romans 6:15–23). That would be like the Allies rescuing one household from the Nazis without also defeating Hitler. Until Hitler is defeated, that household is not really free. Its true freedom is found as part of a bigger picture as a bigger battle is waged against evil.

The *Christus Victor* image of the cross pictures Jesus' overthrow of cosmic powers and authorities in his death (Colossians 2:15), and this overthrow is essential for the redemption of individual sinners. God must rescue us "from the dominion of darkness" to bring believers into Christ's kingdom (Colossians 1:13). This big-picture rescue from the big-picture dominion of darkness does not contradict the message of God's forgiveness of individuals' sins, however, as the next verse demonstrates: in Christ "we have redemption, the forgiveness of sins" (v. 14). The two things go together. But it is essential to see that individual sin is part of a bigger reality: capital-*S* Sin must be overthrown, the evil powers must be conquered, and the dominion of darkness must be plundered of its slaves. Too often evangelicals focus only on the sins of the individual and so miss the wider social and cosmic dimensions of Sin.

Incidentally, this is why many evangelicals tend to be skeptical about social action. Societal issues, such as systemic racism, inequality, misogyny, and so forth, are seen as distractions from the gospel, which is primarily about my sins and Jesus' death for me. Everyone else's greatest need is the same as mine: to have their sins forgiven through Jesus' death. Social issues are viewed as temporary and relatively unimportant compared with one's eternal salvation. As Dennis Edwards notes, "When the gospel is defined as belief in propositions about Jesus in order to validate an individual's personal relationship with God and acquire eternal life, the value given to other human beings is a secondary or tertiary matter, or perhaps does not even exist among an individual believer's list of concerns."[6] But a biblical view of capital-S Sin does not allow such a narrow understanding. Individuals with their personal sins are caught up in bigger systems of oppression that must be overthrown. Paul's message of the cross is that Jesus' crucifixion has turned the world's power systems upside down (1 Corinthians 1:18–31). The cross has critiqued and undermined worldly values as it demonstrates the values of the kingdom of God. And true biblical preaching of the cross must do likewise. There is no simple dichotomy between individual salvation and communal redemption. Edwards adds, "If the gospel we preach does not address the evil that oppresses people, then it is not good news for everyone."[7] Besides that, the Bible is full of concern about social issues. God's care for the oppressed and helpless is an oft-forgotten characteristic of the "tyrannical God of the Old Testament." He insists that his people likewise care for the marginalized (Exodus 23:6, 11; Psalm 82:3; Proverbs

31:8–9; Jeremiah 22:3). As for the New Testament, the apostle James wrote that true religion is "to look after orphans and widows in their distress" (James 1:27). Perhaps this is why the letter of James sometimes does not sit well with evangelicals whose preferences lean more in Paul's direction.

Since the early twentieth century, evangelicals have tended to pit social action against evangelism. But it was not always this way, as Bebbington's history of British evangelicalism shows—with evangelicals leading efforts to abolish the slave trade, for example.[8] It was the 1910 departure of the Cambridge Inter-Collegiate Christian Union (CICCU) from the larger Student Christian Mission (SCM) that set the tone for evangelicals throughout the twentieth century. SCM had accepted higher critical scholarly approaches to the Bible, which CICCU regarded as undermining the status of the Scriptures.[9] After the First World War, SCM unsuccessfully attempted to repair the breach with CICCU, who did not regard the SCM's focus on Christ's atoning death as sufficient,[10] nor their focus on social action in preference to evangelism.[11] Indeed, SCM's theological tendencies became increasingly liberal, and they focused more on social issues than evangelistic preaching. The departure of CICCU from SCM "anticipated the divisions in the wider ecclesiastical world fifteen or so years later."[12] From that point, interest in social action has regularly been interpreted by the theological descendants of CICCU as a sign of sliding into theological liberalism.

But such disregard for social action is an evangelical overreaction. Many British evangelicals before 1910 regarded social action not as a denial of their evangelical faith but as an important expression of it. It did not compromise their crucicentrism.

There is no biblical reason to pit the cross of Jesus against social action as though evangelicalism can spare no resources from one cause for the sake of the other. It's not a zero-sum game. The wider significance of the cross includes its power to critique and undermine worldly power structures. The cross therefore has wide-ranging implications for society at large, not just for individuals who want their personal sins expunged. In any case, the Bible clearly instructs believers to social action. Evangelical biblicism ought to leave the question beyond doubt: social action matters to God and it should matter to evangelicals.

Evangelical disdain for social action may also be motivated, in part, by an unhealthy divide between the sacred and the secular. Though the New Testament affirms a two-kingdom view of this world versus the kingdom of Jesus, it is a mistake to think that God has ceded his claim on this world. It is still his world. So Dutch prime minister and theologian Abraham Kuyper famously quipped, "There is not a square inch in the whole domain of our human existence over which Christ . . . does not cry: 'Mine!'"[13] Christ's kingdom may not be of this world (John 18:36), but he remains nevertheless Lord over all (Colossians 1:15–20). This means that the sacred-secular divide is false. For the Christian, there is no such thing as secular work. All work is to be done "for the Lord" (Colossians 3:23), whatever it is. All so-called secular music, art, literature, and science are ultimately expressions of God's creation. As we engage such pursuits, we employ our God-given minds, hearts, creativity, and intelligence such that the handiwork of the Creator is never absent whether or not we acknowledge his hand in it. It is not possible to divide our lives into secular activities and sacred ones, because they are all sacred. The whole creation belongs to Christ, and we are never outside his service and worship. This means that downplaying the importance of social action (secular) for evangelism (sacred) is grounded on a false dichotomy. When the apostles decided to give priority to the ministry of word and prayer rather than to look after widows, they nevertheless made sure the widows were looked after by faithful and capable people (Acts 6:1–6). Whatever roles each of us may play within the body of Christ, we work together as a team to make sure all the right jobs are done well. It is simply wrong, for a host of reasons, to ignore social action that benefits people's earthly needs.

The Evangelical Gospel

Given what we've said so far, it should come as no surprise that the evangelical gospel is a crucicentric, penal substitutionary, individualistically sin-focused message. And this evangelical gospel can be found in the Scriptures. The problem is that this understanding of the gospel is narrower than the Scriptures'. Joseph Hellerman comments, "The one-sided emphasis in our churches on Jesus as 'personal Savior' is a regrettable example of Western individualism importing its own socially constructed perspective on reality into the biblical text."[14] It is interesting to compare the evangelical gospel with New Testament statements about what the gospel is. Paul describes the gospel of God as "the gospel he promised beforehand through his prophets in the Holy Scriptures regarding his Son, who as to his earthly life was a descendant of David, and who through the Spirit of holiness was appointed the Son of God in power by his resurrection from the dead: Jesus Christ our Lord" (Romans 1:2–4).

This is Paul's most detailed description of the gospel. It is worth noting the gospel's prophetic nature, being foreshadowed in the Old Testament Scriptures. It includes Jesus' "earthly life"—and therefore his incarnation—and his being a descendant of Israel's great king David. It includes reference to Jesus' appointment by the Spirit as "the Son of God in power" through his resurrection from the dead. It is striking how focused Paul's gospel is on Jesus' messianic status. This is the point of his reference to Jesus as a descendant of David, since the promised Messiah was prophesied to be such. Mention of the Spirit likewise relates to Jesus' messianic status, since *messiah* means "anointed one" ("Christ")—someone God has anointed by his Spirit to serve as his appointed king. Furthermore, Jesus' resurrection from the dead is the declaration of his messianic status, for it was prophesied that God's Messiah would not be abandoned to the decay of death (Acts 2:23–36; Psalm 16:8–11). Paul's summary of his gospel is "Jesus is the long awaited Messiah of Israel and Lord of the world."[15]

Ask ten evangelicals to articulate the gospel, and I would bet that fewer than ten would mention Jesus' resurrection from the dead. Fewer than three would refer to the Holy Spirit. And I'd bet that one, or none, would refer to Jesus as the promised Messiah of God. What is up with the evangelical gospel, which suddenly does not seem very evangelical at all if we compare it with Paul's gospel? Paul does not even mention the cross in his most fulsome articulation of the gospel (Romans 1:2–4). He makes no reference to sin and penal substitutionary atonement. To be sure, any particular articulation of Paul's gospel may not include everything he could say. He elsewhere includes the cross in his articulation of the gospel (1 Corinthians 15:1–4). But he does seem content to articulate the gospel without mentioning the cross. And this raises the question as to why evangelicals are so insistent that the cross is the irreducible point of the gospel, especially to the neglect of other elements that Paul emphasizes as part of his gospel, such as Jesus' resurrection and messianic status (Ephesians 3:3–6; 2 Timothy 1:10; 2:8). I guess Paul was not an evangelical.

How the Evangelical Gospel Shapes Evangelical Emphases

It might be ironic, given the theme of this chapter, that the problems inherent to my own evangelical way of reading the Bible were pointed out to me by an evangelical. But it just shows that not all evangelicals fit the stereotype and many can offer critiques of evangelical ways of doing things. Early on in my preparation for Christian ministry, I attended a preaching workshop run by Colin Marshall, an influential voice in Sydney evangelical circles. Since I had never heard Col preach, I somewhat arrogantly wondered what I'd learn from him. As it turned out, I was given a precious insight that has informed my thinking for two decades since.

In preparation for the workshop, we had been asked to create a sermon outline of Mark 2:1–12, Mark's account of Jesus healing a paralyzed man. While chatting about the sermon outlines we'd constructed, Col asked how many of us had made verse 5 the main point of the sermon. This verse is where Jesus tells the paralyzed man, before healing him, that his sins are forgiven. Every person in the workshop put up their hand, because we'd all jumped on the striking reality that upon seeing a paralyzed man, Jesus did not immediately heal him but first forgave his sins. All of our sermons claimed that this passage taught that forgiveness of sins is our biggest need, just as it was this paralyzed man's biggest need. His real need was spiritual, not physical.

Col then asked how many of us gave attention to verses 6–12, in which the teachers of the law complain that Jesus blasphemed by saying he forgives sins, since "who can forgive sins but God alone?" (v. 7). No one put up their hand. We had all pretty much skipped over that part of the passage, or at least we'd subjugated it to the "most important" point of verse 5. Col then told us that he was not surprised. Because evangelicals love to talk about the forgiveness of sins as part of the evangelical gospel, it's not surprising that we all zeroed in on verse 5. But the problem, Col said, was that Mark 2:1–12 is not about that. Forgiveness of sins is in the passage, to be sure. But it's not the main point. The main point is that Jesus demonstrates his divine authority to forgive sins. More than that, he implies that he might be divine himself. That is the main point of the passage, and we had all skipped over it. Why? Because we'd been blinded by our evangelical preferences. The evangelical gospel of forgiveness of sins through the penal substitutionary death of Jesus meant that we could not read the passage properly. The claim of Jesus' divine authority—his divine status—was just not that important to us young evangelical preachers in the making.

I'm grateful for Col's insight and gentle rebuke. He rebuked not only us but also evangelicalism for being so preoccupied with something true that we could not see other things that were also true, even the text's main point. If evangelicals are true biblicists, they must not read the Bible in a way that blinds them to what the Bible says. A preoccupation with *some* things taught by the Scriptures will lead to a distortion of the Scriptures. Of course, evangelicals are not the only ones who are guilty of this, since many theological movements emphasize certain parts of the text and downplay or leave out others. But a central element of evangelical identity is to prize the Bible above all else—evangelicals are the Bible people. If anyone is to avoid letting their agenda dictate how they read the Bible, it ought to be evangelicals. But evangelical emphases guided by the evangelical gospel lead to the same result as other, more overt selective readings; we use the Bible to assert what we want it to say, rather than what it actually says. Tribal readings of the Bible support tribal theology.

IS CHRIST DIVIDED?

In his first letter to the Corinthians, Paul addresses the Corinthians' problematic factionalism. He appeals to the Corinthian believers in the name of Christ that all should agree with one another and there be no divisions among them. They are to "be perfectly united in mind and thought" (1 Corinthians 1:10). It seems that the Corinthians had engaged in some form of hero worship, so that some said "I follow Paul," others "I follow Apollos," and yet others "I follow Cephas [Peter]" (v. 12). Biblical scholar Andrew Clarke suggests that "the Corinthians were aligning themselves with these specific personalities in a personality cult."[16] Ciampa and Rosner claim that this would be "comparable to Christians today aligning themselves with Christian leaders whose reputation has been won through their particular style of preaching," which "brings great potential for inappropriate allegiances to form."[17] Modern evangelical equivalents might be "I follow John Piper" or "I follow Tim Keller" or "I follow Rick Warren." The mention of such leaders is no criticism of them personally, just as Paul does not intend to criticize himself, Apollos, or Peter. The problem is not with the leaders, it is with their followers, who attribute to them such significance that they pit their heroes against others'. Or perhaps more accurate, each regards their hero as the face of their faction or tribe.[18]

This is a normal human tendency; we all seek those who might represent our particular way of looking at the world. But it is not a godly tendency. Paul condemns it, thus even condemning his very own Paul faction. The trouble is that evangelicals often baptize such tribalism because their chosen leaders are godly people who are right about many things. The Piper tribe loves Piper because of his passionate preaching, his zeal for God, and his pursuit of Christian hedonism. But Piper is only human and gets some things wrong. His tendencies and emphases might be adopted wholesale by the Piper tribe, but how helpful is that? How helpful is it if his tribe distinguishes itself from other tribes because their respective leaders hold slightly different views from each other?

But the most insidious faction that Paul condemns is, ironically, the "I follow Christ" faction. Of course Paul wants all of these personality-cult factions to worship Christ alone, so why does he condemn the Christ faction? Simply because Christ is used to divide this faction from the others.[19] And that is the saddest divisive tool available to believers: dividing in the name of Christ. Some evangelicals and ex-evangelicals are guilty of the same thing, and this book could be dangerously close to it too. The Christ tribe rears its head when all the other tribes seem so petty, silly, unnecessarily divisive, and obviously personality driven. The tribe says, "All you other tribes are wrong; only Christ is right." The problem is with the first part of that sentence, not the second. Only Christ is always right, but that does not mean that all the other tribes are wrong. They might be a bit wrong; they might have drifted off into hero worship; they might have erected unhealthy tribal barriers, but surely they're not wrong about everything. The Christ tribe is mistaken about that and so divides off in yet another tribe—in the name of Christ.

Paul's theological ground for condemning Corinthian factionalism is seen in the rhetorical question "Is Christ divided?" (v. 13). Christ is not divided, so there should not be any factions or tribes among Christ's followers. This point foreshadows Paul's extended discussion of the body of Christ in 1 Corinthians 12. The point of that discussion is that Christ's body is one united whole, even though it has different parts. There are distinctions within the body, but there is only one body. Christ's body is not divided. It might have differences within it, and these are healthy and necessary, but such differences do not divide the body's essential unity. Rather, the different parts of the body serve the whole, since the body needs to be more than an eye (12:17). Dividing in the name of Christ always seems at least half right because, well, it is in the name of Christ. That's why the Christ tribe is the most insidious; it is the hardest to spot compared with Piper worship or denomination worship. But Christ is not divided, which means that dividing his followers in his name is always wrong. A much healthier attitude that all evangelical tribes could adopt is the pursuit of unity in Christ. Some evangelical attempts at this, such as Together for the Gospel (T4G) and the Gospel Coalition (TGC), are, I believe, well motivated in this direction. But these coalitions tend to develop their own cultures and tribal characteristics that may just tilt toward creating new bigger tribes.

We won't all agree on everything, and there is organizational wisdom in having likeminded people fellowship together. But there is also wisdom in fellowship with people who don't think the same way. According to historian Doris Kearns Goodwin, Abraham Lincoln's particular genius was his ability to listen to, and learn from, diverse points of view. He assembled a cabinet of people who held diverse views about a great many issues.[20] Wisdom listens to others before making judgment. With humility, wisdom, and patience, it is possible to help each other to see the right. It is possible to persuade. It is possible to change each other's minds. But only if we're talking with each other. Perhaps the worst thing about tribalism is that the tribes stop talking with each other as they spiral deeper into sycophantic echo chambers. Tribes make unity in mind and thought impossible. We will not be persuaded by those whom we have marginalized. We will not listen to those whom we've canceled. We will not see our errors if we listen only to our own tribe.

THE ONE WORD OF GOD

It is sadly ironic that much evangelical tribalism stems from tribal ways of reading the Bible. It is also true that we can make the Bible say just about anything, depending on how we read it. The Bible was used to defend slavery and to support abolition, to support women's suffrage and to condemn it, to affirm democracy and to oppose it. It is used to support Calvinism and its rival Arminianism, to promote Pentecostalism and to reject it, to endorse the politics of the left and the right. With such a diversity of uses, we could be forgiven for thinking there's no point reading the Bible at all. But if Christ is not divided, neither is his Word. The Bible is a unified whole with a coherent overarching message. But like the body of Christ, the unity of the Bible exists in spite of its many parts. The diversity within the Bible is almost overwhelming to the point that many may never glimpse the forest for the trees. Such diversity of eras, cultural backgrounds, languages, and genres makes the Bible the most intriguing, complex, and nuanced literary collection in history. And it is this diversity that enables the manipulation of the Bible to fit almost any agenda—even atheism, since the psalmist can be quoted misleadingly to say, "There is no God" (Psalm 14:1). It is the selection of choice texts, often taken out of context, that enables some interpreters to find biblical support for one view while others find support for its opposite.

The solution to this chaos is first to read and understand the whole Bible. The holistic interpreter is less likely to fall into errors of interpretation of the parts, especially when so many errors are more about balance than straight-up misunderstanding. If some parts, ideas, or themes are emphasized more strongly than they should be, errors ensue. Likewise if other parts, ideas, or themes are underemphasized. All parts, ideas, and themes must be weighed against each other and against the overarching story of the Bible. This story moves from the garden of Eden to the new Jerusalem. It begins with God's creation of the universe with a focus on humanity's special relationship with him. It ends with God's renewed universe with a focus on humanity's renewed relationship with him. The crisis of the story begins with humanity's fall from grace, which is answered by God's long-range plan to redeem humanity to belong to him once again. This plan of redemption first focuses on the nation of Israel, with whom God establishes a covenant replete with obligations of both parties. As Israel fails to uphold her end of the covenant, God promises to make a new covenant that will extend beyond Israel to all nations. This new covenant will be executed through God's chosen servant, who will be installed king over a new kingdom. The Bible presents Jesus of Nazareth as this promised servant-king, whose life, death, resurrection, and ascension fulfill God's promises, inaugurate a new covenant with him, and establish a new kingdom not of this world, constituted of people from every nation, who live in relationship with God through Christ by the power of his Spirit.

There's obviously a lot left out of that summary of the story of the Bible. Different bits and pieces could be included, but the shape of the story is not in doubt. And that means that the Bible is not as open to the wild variety of interpretations we sometimes think. The Bible can be misread by failing to appreciate its overarching story. Every part of the Bible, every chapter and verse, must be read against that story. To begin, it is essential to know where we are in the story when we read the Bible. All those 613 laws and commandments in the Old Testament, for instance, are stipulations of the old covenant for Israel. Today, those in Christ belong to the new covenant, which has its own stipulations. It doesn't mean that everything in the Old Testament is now irrelevant for Christians; quite the contrary. But it does mean that there is no direct line from every part of the Bible to its application today. We must understand what a text meant in its historical context, what it means in its literary context, and where the text fits in the overarching story of the Bible. Only then will we begin to grasp the significance of a text for our lives today.

An understanding of the Bible's story is the single most important tool for getting the Bible right. Once that's in place, readers should then explore the details. And as that exploration happens, we must remember that there is a lot of diversity therein. Sometimes the Bible's diversity includes elements that seem to contradict each other, which is one reason why opposite positions can be argued from it. But knowing that the Bible tells a unified story, it is better to see such elements as standing in a healthy tension with each other. Will life with God be one of blessing or suffering? Yes. Should you waste your time talking with a fool? No. And yes. Should you obey the authorities or rebel against them? It depends. Such tensions reflect the Bible's robust wisdom. Life is not black and white. Our lives are full of healthy tensions, and it is often unwise to resolve them one way or the other. Tribal readings of the Bible fail because they do not give the story of the Bible enough significance, because they read texts out of context, or because they flatten the Bible's many tensions. In his book *Bad Religion*, Ross Douthat argues that all of history's major Christian heresies resulted from flattening one tension or another: "The great Christian heresies . . . all have in common a desire to resolve Christianity's contradictions, untie its knotty paradoxes, and produce a clearer and more coherent faith."[21] For example, is Jesus fully God or fully man? The orthodox answer is yes. So what tensions do modern evangelicals tend to flatten? Here are some suggestions:

- Which is more important, Jesus' death or resurrection?
- Should we live a life of suffering or of triumph?
- Are we saved by faith or by good works?
- Is the Bible the word of God or of man?

- Does our work have eternal value or is it just passing vapor?
- Should we prioritize loving the poor or preaching the gospel?
- Is the kingdom of God here now or not yet?
- Is God a God of unconditional love or of judgment?
- Should we care about the environment or let God take care of it?
- Are all our sins wiped away or will we have to answer for them one day?
- Is our salvation secure in Christ or can a believer fall away?

The Bible's answer to all these questions is yes. If we flatten the tensions inherent to these issues, we will end up misreading the Bible. The tensions are there for a reason, because it's complicated. In our desire to simplify and clarify, we tend to modify. Flattening the tensions in the Bible leads to getting it wrong. Evangelicals ought to be committed to their biblicism above all else in order to be the Bible people. As such, the Bible's complexities and tensions should not be flattened in service of an evangelical interpretive grid. Difficult texts should remain difficult, rather than marginalized. Texts that butt up against the grid should be allowed to reshape the grid. Texts that define the gospel more widely than evangelicals do should have their day in the sun. Then a more theologically robust evangelicalism may flourish. And evangelicals will rightly be able to claim to put the Bible above all other authorities, including evangelical theology itself.

Finally, some epistemological humility will allow evangelicals to resist tribalism. They might see that their tribal boundaries are less defined than they suppose. They might appreciate that other tribes are capable of reading the Bible well. They might even one day remove their tribal walls in the name of a common respect for Jesus and the Bible. We may ask, Why does tribal membership damage our ability to see nuance? Is it failure to listen to people from other perspectives? Is our loyalty to tradition stronger than our loyalty to the text? Are we willing to repent of mistakes? Can we look on "we" only as another sort of "they"?

ONE LOVE

It seems to me that a key impulse driving much tribalism is the desire to be identified as the real deal. The genuine article. A true believer and true worshiper. But Jesus made such identification very simple for his followers. He told them, "By this everyone will know that you are my disciples, if you love one another" (John 13:35). Love for one another is how Jesus' true disciples are known. Love reveals the real deal. Love proves the genuine article. Love is the mark of the true believer and the true worshiper.

The flip side of Jesus' statement is that love erases tribalism. If all true disciples of Jesus are marked by their love for one another, then no competing tribal marker can be legitimate. Who are we to impose theological or cultural barriers that shut others out if they genuinely love Jesus and his followers? Love is the tribal marker that Jesus cares about.

But it's almost too simple, isn't it? We can hardly resist the urge to add nuance, lest Jesus' statement be taken at face value.

Surely only the naïve would do that. What if some of Jesus' followers were to accept theological error even while they love others? Can it really be true that genuine disciples of Jesus are known by this one characteristic?

How we answer that question will reveal much.

FIVE

ACCEPTABLE SINS

You have neglected the more important matters
of the law—justice, mercy and faithfulness. . . .
You strain out a gnat but swallow a camel.

IN 2008, SEATTLE-BASED MEGACHURCH PASTOR MARK Driscoll visited Sydney's Anglican seminary, Moore College, where I was a New Testament professor at the time. Driscoll's visit came at the peak of his popularity, and he electrified evangelicals in Sydney with his brash, retro-hip, hypermasculine persona combined with his humorous, edgy, and often insightful Bible teaching. I admit I was a bit caught up in the hype too, since Driscoll had great success in very secular Seattle and I admired his cultural savvy.

While his 2008 visit ruffled a lot of feathers in Sydney, I witnessed one small moment that colored my view of Driscoll more than anything he said publicly. He had been invited to join the Moore College faculty for lunch before addressing the whole seminary. First, it was a little off-putting that, when he sat down among us, he immediately pulled out his laptop and starting looking us all up on the Moore website. I thought, well, he's doing a quick bit of research about us, but couldn't he have done that before he came? And instead of saying hello and getting to know us a little, he scanned the room and said, "So Graeme Goldsworthy's not here, right?" Driscoll admired Graeme's books and was disappointed to discover that he had retired and was no longer a member of the faculty. I appreciate Graeme too, having been his student and benefited from his publications, so I understood where Driscoll was coming from, though it felt a bit rude.

But what followed next made a deeper impression. After Driscoll closed his laptop, visibly disappointed that Graeme Goldsworthy was not in the room, his assistant hurried in through the door behind Driscoll. The assistant had apparently rushed across the street to buy a Coke for Driscoll and now had a Coke in hand. Then, without turning his head or looking at his assistant at all, Driscoll simply raised his open hand while his assistant approached from behind and placed the Coke in it. Then Driscoll opened the Coke and started drinking. He didn't thank his assistant. He didn't acknowledge his assistant. He didn't even look at his assistant. I found the whole episode weird and unsettling.

Driscoll's brash style of speaking was entertaining. His sharp critique of Sydney Anglicanism could be excused as strong rhetoric to make a point (or eighteen points, in fact).[1] And his provocative handling of the Bible had a way of making people think. But that little interaction (or noninteraction) with his assistant gave me the impression that Driscoll actually was quite arrogant and proud. It didn't look like he treated people with respect. He seemed like a demanding little king who expected his subjects to serve his every whim. Years later, when Driscoll finally resigned as the pastor of the megachurch he had planted, my impression was proved accurate. The church's board had concluded that Driscoll had "been guilty of arrogance, responding to conflict with a quick temper and harsh speech, and leading the staff and elders in a domineering manner" but had "never been charged with any immorality, illegality or heresy. Most of the charges involved attitudes and behaviors reflected by a domineering style of leadership."[2]

The Rise and Fall of Mars Hill, a popular podcast hosted by Mike Cosper, has given wide exposure to these issues.[3] Driscoll's resignation had come after years of complaints about his arrogance from people within his church and from the wider evangelical world. For most of that time, his arrogant and prideful treatment of others had been excused as the minor flaws of a highly gifted and successful church planter. God was clearly blessing his ministry. No one's perfect. Everyone has flaws. Driscoll is a sinner, like everyone else. These platitudes kept more serious responses at bay until Driscoll's leadership style finally became too toxic to manage anymore. But it is interesting to note that the church's board acknowledged Driscoll's arrogance, bad temper, harshness, and domineering leadership, and yet they said that he had "never been charged with any immorality." My question is, What constitutes immorality, then, in their view? Does arrogance not qualify? Does harshness not qualify? Does domineering leadership not qualify? Driscoll can be guilty of all of these things and yet not be guilty of immorality? Seattle, we have a problem.

EVERY TRIBE HAS ITS CODE

This anecdote illustrates a problem in evangelical culture that has long concerned me. The problem is how evangelicals respond to what I would call "acceptable sins." Some sins are patently unacceptable in evangelical culture, such as adultery, homosexual practice, pornography, substance abuse, and divorce. Such things would have got Mark Driscoll fired without much fuss. But arrogance, pride, manipulation, greed, judgmentalism, and divisiveness are not the kinds of sins that create much of a stir. Perhaps they eventually do, as in Driscoll's case, because the situation became untenable, but they are not regarded as fatal flaws that disqualify someone from church leadership.

Evangelicals do regard acceptable sins as sins, just not very serious ones. At least, they are not as serious as the unacceptable sins. Failure or sin that is primarily sexual or related to marriage are given significant weight within evangelical circles. And while evangelical teaching underscores the seriousness of all sin, there is a difference between teaching and practice. There is a difference between official stances and how the culture responds to sin. And the problem with tolerating acceptable sins is that the teaching of the Bible regards the same sins as totally unacceptable. I'm not suggesting that acceptable sins should simply be added to the list of unacceptable sins. I mean that the whole list misrepresents the emphases of the Bible. And as such, it misrepresents what God most cares about. While it is true that the Bible teaches that all sin is serious, it does not give equal treatment to all sin. Just as preachers signal what they think is really important by the amount of time they spend talking about various topics, so the Bible signals what matters most to God through the preponderance of certain recurring themes. Without downplaying the seriousness of evangelicalism's unacceptable sins, the Bible shows that the emphases are misplaced.

UNACCEPTABLE SINS

One year I attended the annual conference of the Evangelical Theological Society in the US and was quite surprised when I met up with a friend and fellow biblical scholar for a drink. We met in a hotel bar, but my friend told me that he could not have an alcoholic drink, else he'd risk being fired from his evangelical university. Just being seen in the bar with me could get him fired, even if he drank only water. I couldn't believe what I was hearing. And no, he was not exaggerating. (I checked.) I understand why Christian institutions might not want their faculty to become drunkards, but banning alcohol altogether? Or firing faculty for partaking in a harmless social occasion with another biblical scholar? From what my friend told me, his university had some real sin problems, such as bullying, disrespect, and dishonesty among its leadership. But drinking water in a bar with a biblical scholar at an evangelical conference is what would get you fired.

Adultery, divorce, homosexuality, abortion, gender dysphoria, drug and alcohol addiction—these are a few of evangelicalism's unacceptable sins. Of course there is no actual list of unacceptable sins. But we know what they are through a set of indicators. The first indicator is that these are all things that get church leaders fired. Second, they are the issues that evangelicals most often rail against. And a third indicator is that these are the sins you can't openly talk about in evangelical churches. Through this set of indicators, and no doubt others too, evangelical culture propagates a vibe around unacceptable sins. While all sin is sin, the vibe can be felt and its message subliminally understood: if you commit these sins, you are basically screwed as a Christian. The pastor will lose his job. The gay Christian will feel like the enemy. And the woman who had an abortion will never reveal her secret shame.

What Gets Church Leaders Fired?

Consider some high-profile cases. Carl Lentz was fired as pastor of Hillsong NYC for infidelity. Tullian Tchividjian resigned from Coral Ridge Presbyterian Church after admitting to an affair. Jack Schaap was fired from First Baptist Church of Hammond for having an affair with an underage girl. (That's also illegal.) Bill Hybels stepped down from leading Willow Creek after accusations of inappropriate sexual advances. What do these recent high-profile cases have in common? Obviously, they all involve sexual immorality. But more to the point is the fact that each of these pastors was fired or resigned immediately once their transgressions became known. The exception is Bill Hybels because he did not confess to the charges against him. When we consider other high-profile cases involving nonsexual failures, however, we see that termination is not immediate. Such cases usually drag on until churches can no longer stomach the toxicity surrounding their leaders.

We've already considered Mark Driscoll at Mars Hill, who had to resign in 2014 because of arrogance, harshness, and a dominating leadership style—*seven years* after complaints about his character were first aired formally by former elders.[4] Similarly,

James McDonald was fired from Harvest Bible Church in 2019 for arrogance, bullying, and divisiveness, among other things—*six* years after former elders wrote to the church board declaring him unfit for leadership.[5] In 2020, Steve Timmis was stood down as CEO of the church-planting network Acts 29 because of bullying and misuse of authority—five years after staff members formally complained about him.[6] These recent high-profile examples of fallen leaders demonstrate churches' and parachurch organizations' slowness to remove leaders who sin in nonsexual ways. The message is clear: sexual sin is unacceptable and will be addressed swiftly. No church leader can survive adultery. But sins such as bullying, arrogance, harshness, and pride are tolerated, at least until such leaders can no longer function. As Scot McKnight and Laura Barringer lament, these abuses express the culture of an institution: "The tragedy of these and far too many other stories is that, instead of focusing on the wounded, the victims, and the survivors of abuse, these organizations focused on themselves, on their leadership, on their own self-interest. They protected the guilty, hid from accountability, and silenced the wounded."[7]

What Do Evangelicals Most Often Rail Against?

Evangelical preaching can signal unacceptable sins directly and indirectly. The direct method involves preaching against sexual immorality, abortion, substance abuse, and other unacceptable sins by condemning them, illustrating the damage they do to perpetrators and victims, and warning of their consequences. The indirect method is to employ lists of unacceptable sins when illustrating the kinds of sins from which Jesus saved believers. Almost without fail, I can predict what sins will constitute these lists. Whenever I hear a sermon that begins to list the sins for which hearers may need forgiveness, I expect internet pornography to be among the first two or three mentioned. Porn always makes the list, but pride usually does not. Lying usually makes the list; arrogance does not. Idolatry, love of money, and lust for material possessions are on the list; gaslighting is not. Being ashamed of Jesus and the gospel is on the list; lacking charity for all is not.

Unacceptable sins are also revealed by evangelical use of social media—the Wild West of ill-formed opinions, unguarded biases, and unreserved trash talk. Church members tend not to wear their Sunday best in this Wild West. Social media, therefore, offers a powerful barometer for what evangelicals really think about a variety of issues, including acceptable and unacceptable sins. It is telling what posts get the most likes, comments, and reposts. An obvious element here is evangelical political activity, which reveals more about unacceptable sins. Evangelicals rail against abortion, but they bemoan Black Lives Matter. They rail against the erosion of religious liberty, but they don't seem too bothered by misogyny. They fight for the Second Amendment, but they don't fight for asylum seekers. If politics were the only indicator, we would conclude that evangelical unacceptable sins are abortion, infringing on liberty, and taking away their guns. Acceptable sins would be racism, inequality, and injustice.

Which Sins Can't You Talk About in Church?

Anyone who's been part of an evangelical church community for more than a few years knows which sins cannot be discussed openly. All sins can be discussed abstractly when they involve people "out there," people we don't know or who are not present. But when it comes to discussion of our own sins and failures, the evangelical insider knows what's not acceptable. Struggling with pornography, for example, is not something a pastor is going to admit from the pulpit during a sermon. He's not going to admit to flirtation with his female colleague. He's certainly not going to admit that his marriage might be on its last legs. Since pastors have a huge influence in shaping the culture of their churches, what they would not confess publicly sets the lead for others to follow.

Most pastors will also not admit publicly to wrestling with doubt. Doubt is a secret unacceptable sin in many evangelical churches, and this was highlighted to me a few years ago when I struggled through a season of doubt myself. I felt I could not admit my doubts to my evangelical academic colleagues, but I did confide in my friend Mark Dever, a prominent evangelical pastor. The reason I could confide in Mark is that he had told me previously that he was "49 percent agnostic." I was a bit shocked that he would admit that and even more so to learn that he had openly said as much to his congregation. The shock of his admission made me realize how taboo doubt was in our circles, and I found his example refreshing and encouraging. It meant that I could talk to him about my own doubt. It also meant that in his church, doubt cannot be a taboo subject because even their beloved pastor experiences doubt from time to time. Mark is the exception that proves the rule that many evangelical churches are not open about doubt. It can be discussed abstractly, perhaps, but most pastors will not admit to it from the pulpit, and most churchgoers will likewise keep their private doubts private.

The example of pastors and the prevailing church culture

means that when regular church folk talk together about their spiritual journeys, they will be careful about what they discuss and with whom. Some sins would not be whispered in a small group Bible study. One to one, they might. I understand that some issues are sensitive and require discretion. Some things probably should not be discussed openly and publicly. But I'm talking about those sins that carry an "evangelical shame tax." They are more heavily weighted because of their unacceptability within the tribe. This is why my marriage failure was a shock to many in our Chicagoland church; a failing marriage was not something that we could talk about openly.

Sins against the Tribe

Some "sins" are unacceptable simply because they go against the tribe. One of my favorite TV shows is *The West Wing*. I love the writing, the characters, and the optimistic vision of what great leadership can look like. It didn't bother me that the president is a Democrat and a Catholic who occasionally rips into evangelical leaders. But years ago, I learned that not all evangelicals feel the same way about this high-caliber TV show. A well-known American biblical scholar once told a friend of mine that "*The West Wing* is not as bad as pornography, but it's close." At the time, I simply could not understand that comment, but now I think I do. The show's idealization of Democratic Party values and its occasional demonization of the Republicans means that few right-leaning American evangelicals could watch it. It's leftist utopian propaganda. It's from the devil.

But *The West Wing* is not from the devil. Just because it is pro-Democrat does not mean that it is opposed to God. American evangelicals' problem with *The West Wing* is that they perceive it to be opposed to their tribe. In the first episode, President Bartlet tells three evangelical leaders to get their "fat asses" out of his White House. I wouldn't be surprised if many evangelicals didn't watch past that. Certainly my American evangelical friend who watched it with me didn't go any farther. In the fifth season, there's also a Bartlet tirade against an antigay evangelical radio personality. So there are a couple of clear denunciations of some evangelical individuals. But it would be a mistake to believe that *The West Wing* is anti-God. To begin, the president is a devout Catholic believer. He regularly draws on his faith throughout his leadership. There's a scene in which he and the First Lady briefly banter about Ephesians 5:21–26 after hearing it preached at church that morning. And there's an episode in which several Chinese evangelicals seek asylum in the United States. In the Oval Office, President Bartlet discusses Christian faith with a leader of the asylum seekers, who perfectly articulates the evangelical gospel, which convinces Bartlet that their faith is genuine. It is a positive and moving portrayal of evangelicals escaping religious persecution. *The West Wing* is not anti-God. It is a bit anti-Republican. But because American evangelicals are so closely associated with the Republican Party, the show goes against the tribe. And because evangelicals often rely on tribal boundaries to determine right and wrong, *The West Wing* is demonized.

Another example is closer to home. I once engaged in a conversation in Sydney about a book that argued against a cherished Sydney Anglican doctrine. The argument was based on biblical and historical evidence. I did not yet have an opinion about the veracity of the argument, but I had no problem that the argument had been mounted. But to establish his case, the author assessed and critiqued the writings of a cherished Sydney biblical scholar.

One of the people I was talking with apparently believed that adjudicating the book was thus a foregone conclusion. "Well, he argues against our Pete, so he must be wrong." I understood the comment as an expression of affection toward our friend, "Pete," but I also believed that the sentiment was probably real. If you challenge a cherished member of the tribe, you'll be opposed whether you're right or wrong. For many evangelicals, opposition to the tribe *is* the evidence that you're wrong.

Going against the tribe is often described as a descent into theological liberalism. Wanting to vote Democrat somehow means you don't believe the Bible anymore. Saying that there is more to Jesus' death than penal substitutionary atonement is a sign of creeping liberalism. Believing that Christians have a duty of care to the poor and outcast means you've left the tribe. Reading the Bible would never lead someone to those conclusions, but they're the kinds of things evangelicals say. Voting Democrat, believing that atonement is bigger than PSA, and caring for the poor are not signs of theological liberalism. They are only signs of resisting tribal values. And opposition to the tribe is one of evangelicalism's biggest unacceptable sins. Sure, it might not constitute a moral failure, like adultery, but it will inevitably tarnish one's evangelical credentials. It will downgrade your status in the tribe. Resisting the tribe is an unacceptable sin because it is the tribe itself that decides what's acceptable and unacceptable.

JESUS, FRIEND AND FOE OF SINNERS

All sin is sin. But it's interesting to note how Jesus interacts with various sinners. His interactions tend to fall into three groups.

First are interactions with people who know they've sinned and feel bad about it. They come to Jesus humbly, sometimes with tears, hoping for comfort. Without exception, Jesus comforts these sinners, is gentle and kind, and makes no mention of their specific sins. Instead, he announces that their sins are forgiven. An example is found in Luke 7:36–50, the passage we discussed earlier in which a sinful woman anointed Jesus' feet with her tears and oil while he visited Simon the Pharisee for dinner. Though Simon condemned the sinful woman—and Jesus for associating with her—Jesus does no such thing. He tells Simon that "her many sins have been forgiven" (v. 47). He tells her, "Your sins are forgiven" (v. 48), and, "Your faith has saved you; go in peace" (v. 50). Other examples like this can be found in passages such as Luke 23:39–43 and John 8:9–11.

Second are interactions with sinners who are relatively neutral toward Jesus, but in the course of their conversation he reveals their sins or shortcomings. They usually acknowledge their failures, and Jesus takes the opportunity to teach them something. He does not condemn them, nor does he rub their noses in it. An example is found in John 4:1–26, which records Jesus' conversation with a Samaritan woman at Jacob's well. After discussing his spiritual living water that wells up to eternal life and her desire for it, Jesus points out that the woman has had five husbands and her current lover is not her husband (vv. 16–18). But rather than focus on her relational failures, Jesus reveals himself to be the promised Messiah (vv. 25–26). Other examples can be found in passages such as Mark 10:17–22, Luke 10:38–42, and John 3:1–15.

Third are interactions with sinners who are hostile toward Jesus and whom Jesus strongly rebukes. These people are guilty of pride, hypocrisy, self-righteousness, or judgmentalism. They are usually religious leaders who perceive Jesus as a threat. They do not repent of their sins, nor does Jesus offer them forgiveness. An example is found in John 8:12–19, in which the Pharisees take issue with Jesus' declaration that he is the light of the world (vv. 12–13). They say his testimony is not valid, while he dismisses their human judgment (vv. 13–15). Jesus' Father testifies for him, but the Pharisees don't know him or his Father. They do not know God (vv. 16–19). Other examples can be found in Matthew 15:1–9, Mark 7:1–13, Luke 13:10–17, and John 8:31–59. This third group of interactions demonstrates what sins Jesus rails against. He harshly rebukes those who are full of pride, those who are hypocritical, those who regard themselves righteous, and those who judge others. Such people are nearly always the religious elite, being Pharisees, Sadducees, scribes, or teachers of the law. They are not humble before others and they take offense at Jesus' welcome of sinners. Of all the ways in which people can fall into sin, surely the sins of this third group are the worst. They are the sins that Jesus rails against. They are the sins for which Jesus offers no comfort or forgiveness. They are the sins that render their protagonists out of relationship with God.

But if all sin is sin, why are these particular sins so bad in Jesus' mind? If we understand the heart of Jesus' teaching and mission, the answer emerges. Jesus preached the coming of the kingdom of God, which requires all to come in repentance and faith (Mark 1:15). Both repentance and faith require humility. Repentance involves a holistic change of direction, while faith is dependence on and allegiance to someone else.[8] It is impossible to do either from a posture of pride. The proud do not like to change their minds. The proud do not easily depend on others. Pride is incompatible with Jesus' message and mission. And that's why sins of pride are so dangerous. God can and will forgive any sin, but only upon repentance and faith. If pride prohibits repentance and faith, no forgiveness is possible.

Notice that the sins of the third group are actually all pride in various forms. Hypocrisy is a false presentation of oneself—while saying one thing, the hypocrite does another. Hypocrites are actors playing a role, fueled by a desire to be perceived by others in a preferred way. So hypocrisy is fueled by pride. Those who regard themselves righteous or are self-righteous believe they are morally superior to others. They look down on the unrighteous and take pride in their own performance. Self-righteousness is an obvious manifestation of pride. Likewise, those who judge others do so from a position of moral superiority. They deem themselves competent to assess the failings of others, and they look down on them rather than empathize with their weakness. Judgmental people see themselves not in the role of the sinner but in the role of God. That's pure pride. There is no more poignant illustration of this than Jesus' parable of the Pharisee and the tax collector in Luke 18:9–14. As we've discussed, Jesus takes direct aim at "some who were confident of their own righteousness and looked down on everyone else" (v. 9). It is the humble and repentant tax collector who "went home justified before God," not the self-righteous and proud Pharisee (v. 14a). The heart of the matter is that "all those who exalt themselves will be humbled, and those who humble themselves will be exalted" (v. 14b). God hates pride. God lifts up the humble.

Jesus impresses the same message upon his disciples during

his last night with them before his crucifixion. Bizarrely, after he has just spoken of giving his body and blood for others (Luke 22:17–20), the disciples debate who among them is the greatest (v. 24). In response, Jesus says they are not to be like pagan kings who lord it over others. "Instead, the greatest among you should be like the youngest, and the one who rules like the one who serves. For who is greater, the one who is at the table or the one who serves? Is it not the one who is at the table? But I am among you as one who serves" (vv. 26–27). Indeed, he will serve by giving his life for the sake of others. And in fulfillment of his promise to exalt the humble, God exalted Jesus "to the highest place and gave him the name that is above every name" (Philippians 2:9). Jesus is not only our greatest example of humility, he shows us that humility is, according to him, one of the greatest human virtues. Humility enables us to see our flaws and failures. Humility enables us to repent and believe. Humility enables us to depend on God's mercy. Humility enables us to put others ahead of ourselves. Humility enables us to forgive the injustices perpetrated against us. And humility is the only antidote for pride, which, according to Jesus, is one of the greatest of all sins.

The Most Biblical Sin

Jesus' view that pride is one of the greatest of sins, if not *the* greatest, finds ample support in the rest of the Bible. Proverbs is an excellent place to start, with the pride-humility dichotomy one of its major themes:

- "He mocks proud mockers but shows favor to the humble and oppressed" (Proverbs 3:34).

- "To fear the LORD is to hate evil; I hate pride and arrogance, evil behavior and perverse speech" (Proverbs 8:13).
- "When pride comes, then comes disgrace, but with humility comes wisdom" (Proverbs 11:2).
- "Wisdom's instruction is to fear the LORD, and humility comes before honor" (Proverbs 15:33).
- "The LORD detests all the proud of heart. Be sure of this: They will not go unpunished" (Proverbs 16:5).
- "Pride goes before destruction, a haughty spirit before a fall" (Proverbs 16:18).
- "Better to be lowly in spirit along with the oppressed than to share plunder with the proud" (Proverbs 16:19).
- "Before a downfall the heart is haughty, but humility comes before honor" (Proverbs 18:12).
- "Haughty eyes and a proud heart—the unplowed field of the wicked—produce sin" (Proverbs 21:4).
- "Humility is the fear of the LORD; its wages are riches and honor and life" (Proverbs 22:4).
- "Pride brings a person low, but the lowly in spirit gain honor" (Proverbs 29:23).

Notice especially Proverbs 16:5: "The LORD detests all the proud of heart." He detests them. That's strong language. And it's reminiscent of Jesus' interactions with the proud of heart.

The pride-humility dichotomy is also prominent in Psalms, as these examples demonstrate:

- "You save the humble but bring low those whose eyes are haughty" (Psalm 18:27).

- "He guides the humble in what is right and teaches them his way" (Psalm 25:9).
- "My sacrifice, O God, is a broken spirit; a broken and contrite heart you, God, will not despise" (Psalm 51:17).
- "Whoever slanders their neighbor in secret, I will put to silence; whoever has haughty eyes and a proud heart, I will not tolerate" (Psalm 101:5).
- "Though the LORD is exalted, he looks kindly on the lowly; though lofty, he sees them from afar" (Psalm 138:6).
- "For the LORD takes delight in his people; he crowns the humble with victory" (Psalm 149:4).

Psalm 18:27 preempts Jesus' teaching that God will exalt the humble and make humble the self-exalted: "You save the humble but bring low those whose eyes are haughty." Jesus' teaching on this is not his own invention but echoes wider biblical wisdom. Several other Old Testament texts lend further support to the theme (1 Samuel 2:1–10; Isaiah 23:9; 57:15; 66:2; Daniel 4:37), but one more poignant example will suffice, from Micah 6:8: "What does the LORD require of you? To act justly and to love mercy and to walk humbly with your God."

What does God require? Justice. Mercy. Humility.

The New Testament likewise shows the importance of humility and the danger of pride. First, Paul:

- "Do nothing out of selfish ambition or vain conceit. Rather, in humility value others above yourselves, not looking to your own interests but each of you to the interests of the others" (Philippians 2:3–4).

- "For by the grace given me I say to every one of you: Do not think of yourself more highly than you ought, but rather think of yourself with sober judgment, in accordance with the faith God has distributed to each of you" (Romans 12:3).
- "Live in harmony with one another. Do not be proud, but be willing to associate with people of low position. Do not be conceited" (Romans 12:16).
- "Love is patient, love is kind. It does not envy, it does not boast, it is not proud" (1 Corinthians 13:4).
- "If I must boast, I will boast of the things that show my weakness" (2 Corinthians 11:30).
- "If anyone thinks they are something when they are not, they deceive themselves" (Galatians 6:3).
- "Be completely humble and gentle; be patient, bearing with one another in love" (Ephesians 4:2).
- "Therefore, as God's chosen people, holy and dearly loved, clothe yourselves with compassion, kindness, humility, gentleness and patience" (Colossians 3:12).

As for the apostles Peter and James, they both show the influence of Proverbs and Jesus' teaching about humility and pride. Peter quotes Proverbs 3:34 and immediately adds what Jesus personally taught him—that God will exalt the humble:[9] "All of you, clothe yourselves with humility toward one another, because, 'God opposes the proud but shows favor to the humble.' Humble yourselves, therefore, under God's mighty hand, that he may lift you up in due time" (1 Peter 5:5–6).

James does the same thing by quoting Proverbs 3:34 and a few verses later reflecting on Jesus' teaching:[10] "But he gives us more grace. That is why Scripture says: 'God opposes the proud but shows favor to the humble.' . . . Humble yourselves before the Lord, and he will lift you up" (James 4:6, 10).

Peter and James were no doubt deeply affected by Jesus' teaching about humility and his example of it, which they embodied in their lives as well as their teaching. And they saw that Jesus echoed Proverbs 3:34—that God is opposed to the proud and shows favor to the humble. Jesus echoed this in his teaching but also in his ministry as he opposed the proud and showed favor to the humble.

Jesus Overturns the Tables on Sin

Just as God will exalt the humble and lower those who exalt themselves, so Jesus turns evangelical assessment of sin upside down. The very sins that Jesus finds most repugnant are the ones that evangelicals tend to excuse. And the sins that evangelicals punish are the ones for which Jesus offers comfort and forgiveness.

All sin is sin. But not all sin is equal. Evangelicals know this, but they have got the weighting wrong, as did their forebears—the teachers of the law and the Pharisees. Jesus accused them of neglecting "the more important matters of the law—justice, mercy and faithfulness" and of straining out a gnat while swallowing a camel (Matthew 23:23–24). This provocative imagery highlights the problem of overvaluing some relatively smaller sins (the gnat) while ignoring comparatively huge sins (the camel). Pride, arrogance, hypocrisy, self-righteousness, divisiveness, judgmentalism, and their ilk are truly deadly sins. Jesus vehemently opposed them. Evangelicals need to stop excusing them and recognize their devastating threat to genuine faith and to the health of believing communities. Evangelicals also need to stop disproportionately demonizing those who fall into the sins for which Jesus offers forgiveness and compassion. If Jesus forgives such sins, why can't evangelicals?

SIX

TILL DEATH DO US PART

*Let any one of you who is without sin be
the first to throw a stone at her.*

THE MOST DISTRESSING AND HAUNTING EXPERIENCE OF MY LIFE
was getting divorced and the horrifying aftermath. Being an
evangelical made it worse than it needed to be. Few issues generate more hurt, damage, and discord among evangelicals than
divorce and remarriage. While other evangelical missteps may
damage the perception of the church or inflict harm on the wider
world, evangelicals mostly hurt themselves with this one. A trail
of hurt and brokenness runs through thousands of churches
because of their attitude toward divorce and remarriage. And
believers will find few faster ways to become alienated by their
own communities than to suffer a marriage breakdown.

WHAT DO EVANGELICALS SAY ABOUT MARRIAGE, DIVORCE, AND REMARRIAGE?

While there are diverse views among evangelicals regarding marriage, divorce, and remarriage, they hold several beliefs in common. Most believe that marriage is a lifelong covenant between a man and a woman and that it is the only appropriate context for sex. It should be ended only by death. Divorce should be avoided at all costs but is permissible in the instances of adultery and desertion. Remarriage of "innocent" divorced Christians is biblical only when their previous marriages were ended by adultery or desertion.

Marriage

Marriage is a great blessing from God, since "it is not good for the man to be alone" (Genesis 2:18). The man and the woman leave their families and "become one flesh" (v. 24), a reference not only to the bonding nature of sex but also to the personal and spiritual union forged between husband and wife. A new family is created, which is the proper context for childrearing, and is bound by a covenant of the highest order. After the fall into sin (Genesis 3), the relationship between the first married couple becomes strained (vv. 12, 16). Genesis 1–3 sets the pattern for all subsequent human marriages. Marriage is a good gift from God but is subject to human sinfulness. As such, marriage is a blessing but will also be difficult as the husband and wife struggle to love each other selflessly.

Marriage is also a dominant metaphor in the Old Testament for God's relationship with his people, Israel. He is the faithful husband who, despite Israel's many infidelities, refuses to divorce his wayward wife (Ezekiel 16). The New Testament transfigures the marriage covenant between God and Israel to Christ and the church (Ephesians 5:22–33). As such, husbands are to be like Christ, offering sacrificial love to their wives (vv. 25–29). Wives are to submit to their husbands as the church submits to Christ (vv. 22–24).[1] The analogy of Christ's "marriage" to the church further raises the stakes of human marriage.

Divorce

Regarding divorce, evangelicals tend to focus on three biblical texts. Malachi 2:16 (supposedly) says that God hates divorce.[2] In Matthew 19:9, Jesus says that anyone who divorces his wife, except for sexual immorality, and marries another woman commits adultery. And in 1 Corinthians 7:10–15, Paul says that believers should not divorce one another, but if an unbelieving spouse leaves, the believer may let him or her go. From Matthew 19 and 1 Corinthians 7, evangelicals normally deduce two legitimate reasons for divorce: adultery and abandonment. While some evangelicals accept other factors leading to divorce, such as physical, emotional, or spiritual abuse, some conservative evangelicals do not accept divorce even under such circumstances.

There is a special dispensation for many who work in church ministry: if they get divorced, they also lose their jobs. This is because pastors are to be "the husband of one wife" (1 Timothy 3:2; Titus 1:6 CSB). Divorcees are regularly disqualified from serving the church in an official capacity.

Remarriage

Even if some divorces are regarded as legitimate, it does not necessarily mean that evangelicals will support the remarriage of a divorcee.[3] Again, this lack of support generally rests on Matthew 19 and 1 Corinthians 7. In the former passage, marriage to someone else after divorce constitutes adultery (Matthew 19:9). In the latter, a wife who leaves her husband must either remain unmarried or be reconciled to her husband (1 Corinthians 7:11). But again, both passages contain an escape clause each: adultery and abandonment. If a husband or wife has been cheated on or has been abandoned, they are free to remarry. If an evangelical remarries apart from these reasons, most evangelicals would not regard the new marriage illegitimate, but they would regard it a sinful act that requires repentance. And remarried people are usually barred from formal ministry, since they fail the "husband of one wife" test of 1 Timothy 3:2 and Titus 1:6.

DIVORCE AND REMARRIAGE IN EVANGELICAL CULTURE

Divorce is always a scandal within an evangelical community, especially if it involves someone in professional church ministry. Even the so-called innocent party can be treated poorly, made to feel guilty over the failure of their marriage, and barred from any meaningful role within the church. Because divorce is one of the most painful and stressful experiences a person could endure, it is doubly tragic when the church fails to love, care for, and encourage divorcees. And it is even worse when guilt, shame, and harassment are piled on instead.

My own experience of divorce was very difficult and was made worse by some of the people in my life—who would soon no longer be in my life. Some of my evangelical (now former) friends blamed me for the end of the marriage because they listened to only one side of the story, and most did not bother to hear my side of the story or to see whether I was okay. Some condemned me behind my back; others harassed me on Facebook; still others just acted as though I no longer existed. For years I had downplayed complaints about judgmental Christians because I thought such people were the minority who misrepresented the heart of the church, which was full of love and mercy. Unfortunately, I learned that Christians can be very judgmental. At times I wondered whether they really believed in a merciful, loving God, or thought of divorce as an unforgivable sin.

Following my separation, I attended the evangelical church where I had become a Christian twenty-five years before and where I had served as an associate pastor a decade later. But after a year or so, I could not continue attending that church. I constantly felt the stigma of my failed marriage, and I felt uncomfortable as one half of the couple they'd known for more than two decades. I'm sure a lot of this was in my head, but I also felt like I was under suspicion, and there was little effort to put me at ease. No one invited me to their home for a meal, few asked how I was coping, and some of the preaching just made me feel more guilty. I remain grateful for all I learned in that community and for the encouragement I received as a young believer. And no church is perfect. I'm not offering my experience to critique this particular church but to illustrate something that I believe is typical among evangelical churches. Many evangelical divorcees end up leaving their churches for other churches or they leave church altogether.

As I write this, I can imagine various responses to my painful experiences. Some will say I brought it on myself by getting divorced. Others will wonder whether I'm even a Christian anymore, since I got divorced, remarried, and now am writing a book critiquing evangelicalism. And yet others will recognize the problems I'm articulating and will pray for the damaged and hurting believers in their midst. They may also pray for a renewed culture within the church that seeks to share the love of God in Christ even to those who have failed in the most spectacular fashion.

There were some notable exceptions, friends who responded to me with love, care, and grace. A stellar example was Paul Dale, an Anglican minister in Sydney, who proved himself a true friend and minister of God's love. Unlike many others, he had known of the significant troubles in my marriage for fourteen years leading up to the divorce, and he knew that we had done all we could to save the marriage. He did not tell me to "just fix it," and he encouraged me to avoid guilt and shame and rather to trust in the fatherly love of God. He helped to get me through the most difficult year of my life, and he helped me to remain a Christian when others were provoking me to despise the church.

What Are the Biblical Grounds for Your Divorce?

The response of one evangelical friend upon hearing of my separation typifies that of many evangelicals. Instead of asking what had happened or how it had come to this or how I was doing, his first question was, "What are the biblical grounds for your divorce?" His main concern was whether this would be a biblically acceptable divorce. If not, I was fairly certain, he would feel justified to rebuke me and refuse to accept it. I understand where this attitude comes from, because my friend desired to honor God and to make sure I was not going astray. I may have even said something similar myself once or twice in years past. But now that I was in the getting-divorced seat, this question felt pastorally and personally insensitive, to say the least. The "divorce-acceptability diagnostic" invites argument over texts, interpretation, and application rather than caring for someone in need. Even though I could run circles around my friend on that front, doing so would have felt like I was just being defensive or self-justifying or like special pleading. In any case, I picked up a clear vibe that it would not have mattered what I said to defend myself. I was guilty, and no amount of Bible gymnastics would change that.

No one wants their marriage to end. My ex-wife and I had been committed Christians for two decades and wrestled through our difficulties to try to make the marriage work. The crisis of separation did not occur lightly and it did not happen overnight. I had prayed every day for five years that it would not happen. The abrupt and challenging divorce-acceptability diagnostic was not what I needed at that time. I was well past such considerations. I was hurting, my life was falling apart, and my world was burning down. Questions like this only reinforced my experience of evangelical culture as merciless, combative, and self-righteous around the issue of divorce.

Who's to Blame?

Another unhelpful dynamic to some evangelical responses to divorce is the attempt to pin the blame on one party. The impulse to do so arises not necessarily from gossipy voyeurism but from the biblical texts. Both Matthew 19 and 1 Corinthians 7 point to a guilty party who triggers an acceptable divorce through either their adultery or abandonment. To be sure, there will at times be a guilty party who commits adultery or abandons their spouse. But in many cases of divorce, there is no single guilty party. More realistically, there are two guilty parties in every divorce. And if the reason for divorce is not adultery or abandonment, it becomes unclear who that guilty party is or even why it is important to figure that out.

Most divorces simply recognize something that has already happened: the marriage has died. Divorce doesn't kill marriages. It buries them. They're already dead. But some Christians don't want to admit that the marriage died through a complex of causes and events. They'd rather position themselves as the innocent party to avoid being stigmatized by the community, and so they will be free to remarry without too much hassle. In reality, however, they are likely to face stigma whether or not they are perceived as the innocent party. The other reality is that even when there is a clearly guilty party, that does not mean the other person is innocent. As a counselor told a friend whose wife cheated on him, the adultery is on her, but the state of the marriage that led to it is on both of them.

None of this is to exonerate someone clearly guilty of breaking their marriage vows, though we should remember that even such a person is not beyond God's mercy and forgiveness. But it recognizes that marriage breakdown is usually more complex than that, and it can happen without adultery or abandonment. Evangelicals would do better not to speculate, make judgments, or gossip. A divorcing couple might choose to confide in a few close friends and family members, their pastor, and their counselor. Everyone else should pray for them and mind their own business.

Judgment and Alienation

Those who get divorced in an evangelical context are likely to experience some form of judgment and alienation. This is often one of the factors that keeps evangelicals from divorcing in the first place: they are afraid of the judgment that will follow. And the stigma of divorce is strong enough that, regardless of the motives or details behind the divorce, divorcees will still carry a dark cloud over their heads. I was glad to have family and many non-Christian friends when I got divorced, simply because they didn't judge me. They also didn't distance themselves. The most supportive communities in the face of my personal tragedy were not Christian ones. Some evangelicals will argue that this is because non-Christians don't care about marriage as much as we do, so their lack of judgment is cheap. Unbelievers might even celebrate your personal freedom and ability to do whatever you want. None of that is very Christian. But these arguments serve only to excuse the very real problem of evangelical judgmentalism.

While a few evangelical friends drew nearer in my time of crisis, many kept their distance. Some of that was intentional, while some of it was just neglect because of awkwardness. Perhaps they didn't know what to say, felt embarrassed for me, or just found the situation sad and uncomfortable. Reading between the lines, together with one or two open conversations, helped me to see that most believing friends found my divorce too hard to deal with. So they kept away.

Adding Economic Stress to Personal Tragedy

As someone who has worked in professional Christian service or been training for it since age twenty-one, I had an additional pressure to keep my marriage together: I knew that I could lose my job and that all that I'd done over more than twenty years would come tumbling down. For years I worried about how I would financially support my family if I lost my job because of marriage failure. A difficult marriage is stressful for anyone, but doubly so for evangelicals because of the fear of judgment. And triply so for anyone whose economic viability is tied to their marriage. On reflection, I think the added pressure made it more difficult to resolve some of the issues in my marriage.

A friend in Chicago lost his position as pastor of a church that loved him, because his wife left. He didn't want the divorce, he didn't instigate it, and he didn't break his vows. But he could no longer lead the church because his marriage was over. After years of rigorous theological study, tireless efforts in service of the church, and wonderful preaching, he ended up working at McDonald's. It doesn't seem to matter what factors lead to the marriage break. Whatever the reasons, that pastor is suddenly unfit for service and will normally lose their job. While that pastor's family is being torn apart and their lifelong covenant is breaking, the church adds economic stress to the situation, not to mention the public humiliation and emotional distress of being removed from leadership of the people for whom you have poured out your heart. Theological students, be warned: If your marriage is not absolutely rock solid, you should rethink training for ministry. The pressures of ministry will crack your vulnerable marriage open and you'll be fired from ministry.

WHAT DOES THE BIBLE SAY ABOUT MARRIAGE, DIVORCE, AND REMARRIAGE?

The Bible has much to say about marriage, divorce, and remarriage. But we need to apply more of the Bible to those topics than the passages that directly address them. We also need to consider God's heart, Jesus' compassion, and the meaning of marriage. The Bible's teaching about who God is, who we are, and how the two relate is key to any biblical discussion of, well, anything.

Evangelical thinking tends to look at all the relevant passages, put them together, and compile a list of what God says about something. This is how we arrive at the "two legitimate reasons for divorce" type of thinking. But we must always remember that the Bible is not a volume of systematic theology. It does not lay out its teaching in neat categories according to subject and logic. Every part of the Bible is written within its historical context, addressing the needs and concerns of its time. Of course much teaching in the Bible involves universal claims that transcend these contexts, needs, and concerns, but such universal claims cannot simply be derived from the biblical texts without consideration of their complexities. Each text must be handled carefully before it can be plumbed for its universal relevance. And even after that work is done, we need to figure out how it relates to the big themes of the Bible, which primarily involve who God is and how we can know him. The following discussion offers an attempt to do some of this (it can't be done in full here) to give a clearer picture of what the Bible says about marriage, divorce, and remarriage. I won't repeat the discussion of biblical texts I've already offered, but I will supplement it as needed.

Marriage

When Genesis 2 establishes the biblical bedrock for marriage, it is sometimes forgotten that marriage is meant for the *good* of husband and wife. It is for a physical and spiritual union of the two. It addresses the need for companionship. All of these things are implied by the text, if not stated directly.[4] We should be sensitive to the important things a text says without saying them, and though the Bible places great importance on marriage, it needs to be remembered that it is meant primarily for the good of both parties. This point is important to remember when a marriage goes bad. Of course it would be better if all marriages were healthy and great. But they're not, are they? So it doesn't really help just to say they should be something they're not. When a marriage deteriorates to the point of doing ongoing harm or degradation to one or both parties, it can no longer be regarded as fulfilling the purpose of marriage.

And let's not forget that Genesis 3 sets the pattern for difficulties in marriage. The human fall into rebellion against our Creator means that all relationships are fraught with potential danger, and marriage is no different. If anything, Genesis 3 should set our expectation that a fair number of marriages will simply not make it. And we should note that the Bible never promises that a Christian marriage will make it. While Jesus came to undo the fall, we live with its effects still. Several promises are made in the Bible, but a successful Christian marriage is not one of them.

The use of marriage as a metaphor for God's relationship with Israel, or Christ's relationship with the church, is very powerful for understanding how God relates to us, but we should avoid misapplying the imagery. That God made a marriage covenant with his people does not mean that in human marriage we are making a covenant with God. Marriage is a covenant made between two fallen individuals, not with God. We may say our vows *before* God, who witnesses our promises, but the covenant is not *with* God. This is important to remember when faced with marriage failure. If we think our marriage is a covenant with God, then its failure will spell the end of our relationship with him too. But that's simply not the case. As Paul says, nothing in all creation can separate us from the love of God in Christ (Romans 8:38–39), and that includes a failed marriage.

The marriage metaphor puts pressure on Christian marriages in another way too. Evangelicals often say that the true meaning of marriage is to point to the relationship between Christ and the church (Ephesians 5:22–33). Ephesians 5 does seem to imply that the ultimate significance of human marriage is its correlation to the union between Christ and the church.[5] This point is then leveraged to emphasize the dramatic importance of marriage. If a marriage fails, it will somehow compromise Christ's relationship with the church. That's a lot of weight to put on someone's marriage. A Christian may think that divorce is just as inconceivable as Christ divorcing his people. But that kind of reasoning is illogical. Many things in God's creation point to something beyond themselves. But if the signpost is less impressive than the thing it points to, we don't scold it for being a bad, nasty signpost. No, we say, "Look at what it's pointing to!" Take parenthood, for example. It points us to the fatherhood of God. But when someone is a bad parent, we don't worry that the fatherhood of God is somehow compromised or besmirched. Instead, we do the opposite. We say, "You may have had a crap father, but your Father in heaven will never let you down."

"Maybe your parents didn't love you, but God's love never fails." Ugly signposts point as surely to their destination as beautiful signposts do. To be sure, a beautiful marriage will be a lovely witness to the union between Christ and his church. And a bad marriage will remind us how special and unusual it is.

Divorce

In Malachi 2:16, God does not say, "I hate divorce."[6] Some older translations (the King James Version) rendered the tricky Hebrew this way, but recent translations (New International Version, Christian Standard Version, English Standard Version) do not, reflecting the consensus of modern evangelical scholarship. The ubiquitous NIV translation reads, "'The man who hates and divorces his wife,' says the Lord, the God of Israel, 'does violence to the one he should protect,' says the Lord Almighty. So be on your guard, and do not be unfaithful." Malachi warns of faithlessness in marriage, through which an abandoned wife was susceptible to homelessness and poverty in the ancient setting. As Michael Floyd comments, Malachi assumes "that divorce of some sort is a legal option, and neither prohibits nor condemns divorce outright." Rather, he "attempts to persuade the people of Judah to take care of their marriages and not to let the bonds of affection between husband and wife deteriorate, so that they will not resort to divorce lightly."[7] But Malachi does not say that God hates divorce. That mistaken translation has caused much grief and confusion for believers who have suffered divorce.

Evangelicals' two reasons for divorce come from Matthew 19 (or Mark 10) and 1 Corinthians 7, but it is possible to see flawed logic at play once we read the two passages together. In Matthew 19:9, Jesus says that anyone who divorces his wife and marries another commits adultery, except when sexual immorality has been a factor in the divorce. According to this reading of Jesus' words, apart from cases of sexual immorality, any remarriage is adultery. But Paul apparently contradicts this view, since he says that believers who are abandoned by their spouse are "not bound in such circumstances" (1 Corinthians 7:15). Many commentators agree that "not bound" means that Paul believes that divorce and remarriage are both permissible in such situations.[8] So Paul's second acceptable reason for divorce seems to contradict Jesus' view that no remarriage is acceptable apart from cases of adultery.

Evangelicals prefer to harmonize apparently contradictory texts rather than concede that a contradiction exists. And such harmonization between these two texts is possible once we dig into both a little more. In Matthew 19, some Pharisees seek to trap Jesus by raising a contentious issue that had divided Jewish thinkers: divorce.[9] They ask Jesus whether it is lawful to divorce one's wife "on any grounds" (v. 3 CSB). "On any grounds" was a catchphrase in a debate on how to apply Moses' words in Deuteronomy 24:1:[10] if a wife becomes displeasing to her husband because he finds "something indecent" about her, he may write her a divorce certificate. Within contemporary Judaism were two competing schools of thought on the issue. The school of Rabbi Hillel focused on the "something." Anything that provoked the husband's displeasure, such as ruining a dish or finding a prettier woman, could be grounds for divorce.[11] The school of Rabbi Shammai, however, focused on the "indecency." The wife had to be guilty of some sort of moral indecency to warrant divorce. We should assume this meant not adultery, which automatically led to divorce, but some other violation, such as talking to men or loosening her hair in public.[12] Jesus sidesteps this debate and the Pharisees' trap by going straight to God's intent for marriage as seen in Genesis 1:27 and 2:24: "'Haven't you read,' he replied, 'that at the beginning the Creator "made them male and female," and said, "For this reason a man will leave his father and mother and be united to his wife, and the two will become one flesh"?'" (Matthew 19:4–5).

Jesus then reflects on the implications of these texts (especially Genesis 2:24), commenting that the married couple are now one flesh, and "what God has joined together, let no one separate" (Matthew 19:6). To which the Pharisees object, asking why then did Moses permit divorce (v. 7)? Jesus then explains how Moses' concession fits with the creation ordinance he has just cited from Genesis 1 and 2: "Moses permitted you to divorce your wives because your hearts were hard. But it was not this way from the beginning" (v. 8).

Evangelicals will sometimes interpret Jesus' words here to mean that his own teaching supersedes Moses', which would not be out of character in Matthew's Gospel. But Jesus employs an established method of argumentation that held sway in Jewish thought, whereby appeal to first principles sets the table for interpreting following principles. He is not setting one Scripture against another but showing that Genesis 2 establishes the ideal intention for marriage. Moses' divorce concession in Deuteronomy 24 is a regrettable but necessary provision for our failure to maintain the ideal.[13] Or to look at it another way, Genesis 2 is pre-fall, while Deuteronomy 24 addresses a necessity arising from the fall of Genesis 3. The "hardness of your hearts" that Jesus says undergirds divorce points directly to Genesis 3. Fallen human hearts are often not able to maintain God's ideals.

Putting this together, I would say that Jesus affirms the sanctity of marriage in the strongest possible terms, but he also acknowledges that human failure must also be accommodated. The school of Rabbi Hillel was certainly wrong to allow divorce for any reason. The creation intent for marriage ought to be affirmed, making divorce a regrettable last resort, not subject to whim or fancy. (I'll comment on Matthew 19:9 in the following section on remarriage.)

As for 1 Corinthians 7, Paul addresses matters that the young Corinthian church wrote to him about (v. 1), which evidently included the issue of marriage to an unbeliever. As a young church, many of the new believers in Corinth were already married to people who did not yet believe. Though Paul counsels believers to marry other believers (v. 39), an existing mixed marriage is legitimate (v. 14). As such, the believer should not divorce the unbeliever if they are willing to stay in the marriage (vv. 12–13). But, Paul says, if the unbeliever leaves the marriage, "let it be so" (v. 15a). Divorce is permitted and the believer "is not bound in such circumstances" (v. 15b). The logic underpinning this instruction appears in the final clause of verse 15: "God has called us to live in peace." No one can force someone else to be married to them. Or if they attempt to do so, the inevitable separation will likely be acrimonious. The believer, on the contrary, is to favor peace and let the marriage go if need be.[14]

Though Paul addresses a specific situation in which already married people come to faith while their spouses do not, I see no reason why Paul's logic does not apply also to marriages in which both parties are believers. After all, Paul simply imagines one reason why a spouse might want to leave the marriage, given the issue he was asked about: their spouse has become a believer.

But it is obviously not the only reason why a spouse might want out of a marriage, even a believing spouse. Perhaps the marriage is acrimonious for other reasons, such as prolonged abuse, degradation, or betrayal of various kinds. Whatever the reason, once a spouse needs to exit a marriage, the other should "let it be so." And this is for the same reason as before: "God has called us to live in peace." Christians should not hold each other captive in a failed marriage just because they're Christians. Obviously, every attempt should be made to save the marriage, but we must accept the reality that not all marriages can be saved (as a result of Genesis 3). Once it's over, let peace reign.[15]

There is another reason why this text should not be understood too narrowly. Wayne Grudem, a conservative evangelical theologian, has shown that the phrase "in such circumstances" (the believer "is not bound in such circumstances," v. 15) refers to a wider set of possibilities than is mentioned in the text. After surveying the use of the original Greek phrase across ancient Greek literature, Grudem demonstrates that it usually refers to a wider pool of examples than those mentioned in the text. This means that when Paul says that believers are not bound "in such circumstances," this could apply to other situations besides the one explicitly cited in the text: when an unbelieving spouse exits the marriage. Grudem concludes, against his teaching on the subject for decades, that there were other reasons why Christians could legitimately divorce, such as in the case of abuse.[16]

My reading of Matthew 19 and 1 Corinthians 7 leads me to reject the traditional evangelical view that there are only two legitimate grounds for divorce: adultery and abandonment. Jesus acknowledges that Moses' divorce concession is necessary because of human sin. Paul acknowledges that, in the interest of peace, believers are not bound to a marriage that has gone bad. Of course both Jesus and Paul affirm the sanctity of marriage and regard divorce as a regrettable concession to the ideal. But it is a concession that is sometimes needed because of our fallen humanity and in the interest of peace.

The loss of a job because of divorce for people in Christian ministry stems from a misunderstanding of 1 Timothy 3:2 (and Titus 1:6). In 1 Timothy 3:1–13, Paul lists some of the characteristics that would qualify someone to become an overseer of a church (vv. 1–7) or a deacon (vv. 8–13). An overseer must be "the husband of one wife" (v. 2 CSB), which is interpreted to mean that divorced people or those who are divorced and remarried are disqualified from leadership. But literally the Greek text describes an overseer as a "one-woman man." And this probably does not mean that the candidate has been married only once. For instance, it is hard to accept that Paul would ban from leadership a widower who remarried after his first wife died. What would be the point of such a disqualification? Even evangelicals allow remarried widows and widowers to do ministry. So "one-woman man" likely does not mean that the leadership candidate has only ever been married to the one spouse. In that case, the alternate way of interpreting the phrase is most likely that a "one-woman man" is someone who is faithful to his wife and not a polygamist.[17] The point is faithfulness, not the number of marriages. This makes better sense of the passage as a whole, which identifies characteristics that make a person suitable to lead a church. If someone commits adultery and so ends their marriage, they would be disqualified from leadership according to 1 Timothy 3:2. But if a marriage ends for other reasons, 1 Timothy 3:2 does not speak to whether a person is fit for leadership in the church.

Remarriage

The biblical foundation for marriage is found in Genesis 2, as Jesus affirms in Matthew 19, and the key reason provided there is that "it is not good for the man to be alone" (Genesis 2:18). We could assume, therefore, that if a divorce is legitimate, then remarriage ought also be legitimate. After all, why should someone remain alone because their marriage failed? On top of the anguish and disappointment of a failed marriage, the believer is condemned to remain single for the rest of their life. But many evangelicals don't see it that way. They claim that even if a divorce is legitimate, the divorced person must remain single.[18] Again, Matthew 19 and 1 Corinthians 7 are the key texts used to support this view. This time we'll look at 1 Corinthians 7 first, then Matthew 19.

Paul says that a wife must not separate from her husband, but if she does, she must remain unmarried or be reconciled to her husband (and vice versa, 1 Corinthians 7:10–11). Out of context, this sounds as if Paul forbids remarriage. But the astute reader will realize that this seems to contradict what Paul says later in the passage, as we've already addressed: in such situations in which a marriage has failed, the believer is not bound but should seek peace (v. 15). But the two instructions are easily correlated the same way that Jesus correlated Genesis 2 with Deuteronomy 24:1: there is an ideal, and there is a concession to the ideal. Paul instructs married people to stay together. But he also concedes that sometimes that will not be possible. In such circumstances, the believer is not bound, meaning that not only is the divorce permissible but so is remarriage. It would be draconian to insist that "unbound" means freed from the bad marriage but not free to remarry. As we will explore in a moment, there was no ancient view of divorce that did not permit remarriage.

In Matthew 19, Jesus is speaking into a specific context, as we've already seen. The school of Rabbi Hillel taught that a man could divorce his wife for any reason and be married to another. Jesus straight out rejects such a cavalier attitude to marriage and states that anyone who divorces his wife, apart from sexual immorality, and marries another commits adultery (v. 9). Taken out of context, this sounds like Jesus is saying that any subsequent marriage is adultery (unless the first marriage ended because of adultery). But with the school of Hillel in the background, Jesus regards the casual discarding of a wife for another as adultery, since the man should not have discarded his wife in the first place. Without a legitimate reason for divorce, a subsequent marriage is adultery. But we should remember that Jesus has already affirmed Moses' divorce concession in verse 8. Divorce is not the ideal (Genesis 2), but it is sometimes necessary (Genesis 3). Many men in Jesus' day, following Rabbi Hillel, were divorcing their wives illegitimately, failing to acknowledge the ideal of Genesis 2, let alone live up to it. Jesus' overall purpose is to reaffirm the ideal of marriage, not to set up only one legitimate ground for divorce. A casual abandonment of one wife for another is adultery. But there are legitimate reasons for divorce because of human failure.

Finally, the idea that a divorce might be legitimate but remarriage might not is foreign to the historical context of the Bible. Biblical scholar Craig Keener notes that "a valid divorce by definition included the right to marry, as is attested by ancient divorce contracts."[19] As another biblical scholar, David Instone-Brewer, has revealed, "Jews and Romans in the first century thought that most divorcees *should* remarry. . . . Remarriage for divorcees in the first century was therefore the norm—if they did not do so they were contravening the secular or religious law."[20] This universal understanding in the ancient world further reinforces the interpretation of Jesus' words. He condemns not all remarriages, in clear denunciation of the universal understanding and legal obligations of his time, but only those in which a wife is hastily abandoned for another. To do so would be adultery.

A BETTER WAY

Judgmentalism is never a good look for the church. But evangelicals seem especially prone to judgmentalism on the topic of divorce and remarriage. Instead of caring for hurt and suffering people, some evangelicals shoot their wounded. But this was not Jesus' attitude toward hurting people. While he had some strong things to say about marriage and divorce, he showed no trace of judgmentalism when he encountered those who'd failed in this area, such as the Samaritan woman who'd had five husbands (John 4:1–26). Surely, our first response toward those who've experienced personal tragedy, failure, or betrayal ought to be compassion and comfort. Even if you hold a conservative view on divorce and remarriage, a judgmental spirit is not going to help anyone. It will just increase guilt and shame while turning brokenhearted believers against the church.

Caring for the Divorced

Christians don't always know what to say to those who've experienced brokenness in their marriages. The gravity of the issue can make it hard to say something that doesn't make them feel worse than they already do. It's similar to responding to the grief of losing a loved one. Christians sometimes say unbelievably unhelpful things, like "it must have been God's will for her to die." Far better to have a couple of phrases up your sleeve, like "I'm so sorry for your loss. I know you loved him very much." Such remarks do not offend anyone, and they acknowledge the grief being experienced. Knowing ahead of time what to say and what not to say can really help.

When a friend or family member shares news about their separation or divorce, it is helpful to say, "I'm so sorry. Are you okay? Do you want to talk about it?" Avoid asking questions like, "What are the biblical grounds for your divorce?" "Who's to blame?" or, "Is there someone else?" Whether or not you think the divorce is legitimate, it's important first to acknowledge the personal and emotional gravity of the situation. Let them know you care. Let them know their relationship with you is not at risk. Let them know they're accepted and safe with you. Then, and only then, you might inquire about the details of the situation, but only if your friend wants to talk about it. It's entirely possible they don't, and that doesn't mean they're hiding something. It can be upsetting, retraumatizing, and exhausting to talk. Understand that. Offer an ear and a shoulder. Offer prayer. Offer practical help. If they want to confide in you, fine. But it's not your job to gather evidence for your inner juror to decide the legitimacy of their divorce.

If someone in your church has gone through divorce or is going through it, don't let them feel like a pariah. Talk to them. Include them in your group. Smile. Even a regular level of disinterest might be interpreted as a snub, because they expect believers to be judging them. If you're the pastor, make a point of being seen talking with the divorcee after church. Remind your parishioner that God loves them and that nothing can get in the way of his love, not even divorce. Be a model of a loving, accepting community. Churches can even establish support groups for divorced people, like Divorce Care at Village Church in Annandale, Sydney. Not only are such groups extraordinarily helpful for sufferers of broken marriages, they communicate a healthy and caring posture toward the brokenhearted from which the church at large can learn. They can even provide an effective way to connect with unchurched folk in the neighborhood.

Loving the Remarried

Those who've been remarried after divorce are often made to feel like pariahs too. It can be tricky for friends and family to support a remarriage, even if they support it in theory. They might be grieving the broken marriage or find it weird to see their friend with a new spouse. Your willingness to embrace the new marriage and new spouse will determine the future of your friendship. If you can't embrace the marriage, say goodbye to your friend. They've formed a new primary allegiance, and their new marriage is more important than your friendship. If you reject the marriage, you're rejecting your friend. But if you want to keep your friend in your life, allow me to offer some suggestions. Get over your grief and awkwardness. Embrace the new spouse. Befriend him or her. Invite the new couple over for dinner. Acknowledge the legitimacy of their marriage. And do all you can to help them to thrive in their new life together.[21]

Church Leadership

Churches should not adopt a stance on divorce and remarriage within the church leadership that is based on simplistic readings of a few texts. When Paul addresses the matter, his main concern is faithfulness, and it should not be assumed that every divorced person is unfaithful somehow. To be sure, some cases will be more clear-cut than others, but churches would do well to avoid thoughtless legalism that misrepresents the intention of the biblical texts and does not show proper care toward divorced leaders.

It should also be recognized that when Paul wrote to Timothy and Titus about the qualifications for church leaders, he offered a diagnostic for *untested* potential leaders. If a pastor has successfully led his church for thirty years before his marriage fails, a different measure is needed. Churches should avoid knee-jerk reactions that regard the pastor as suddenly unfit for the role they've already successfully executed for decades. Instead, churches should consider how they can care for their pastor now. How can they apply the love of God to the one who has applied it to them for years? How can they exercise mercy and grace to the person who's taught them about God's mercy and grace? How can they sustain the servant whose marriage has sustained the wounds of service? How can they pray for the one who has tirelessly upheld them in prayer for so long?

The common evangelical approach to divorce and remarriage further demonstrates the problems that come from simplistic readings of biblical texts. And judgmental, unloving Christians betray the spirit and character of Jesus—let the one without sin cast the first stone (John 8:7)—not to mention his gospel of mercy and love. It's little wonder that many divorced Christians eventually become disillusioned with the church, but it need not be that way.

SEVEN

MEGAPERCH PASTORS

Whoever wants to become great among
you must be your servant.

THE HARTFORD INSTITUTE FOR RELIGION RESEARCH DEFINES a megachurch as a Protestant church with a sustained weekly attendance of two thousand or more people. Though very large congregations have existed in earlier eras, such as Charles Spurgeon's six-thousand-seat Metropolitan Tabernacle, founded in London in 1861, today there are about 1,750 megachurches in the US, after a steep incline in their number since the 1970s.[1] On one weekend in 2015, one in ten Protestants in America—approximately five million people—attended a megachurch service.[2] According to a study by the Hartford Institute published in 2020, American megachurches have an average weekly attendance of more than four thousand people and an average of 7.6 services per weekend, and 70 percent of megachurches have a multisite network.[3] Megachurches are not the exclusive domain of evangelicals, but since 65 percent of megachurches are evangelical in theology and 40 percent are nondenominational,[4] their association with evangelicalism is clear.

Most megachurches follow a similar growth pattern. They grow quickly within a short period—usually less than ten years—under the leadership of one senior pastor, who is normally a white male with unusual personal charisma and of an average age of fifty-three. As the church grows, the senior pastor is supported by dozens of associate ministers along with an ever-growing full-time staff. This may last for a decade or two, though few megachurches remain very large following the tenure of the original pastor.[5]

A popular perception is that megachurches are especially good at attracting the unchurched. Willow Creek, for example, was known for its profile of "Unchurched Harry" as their ideal or typical target recruit.[6] But research shows that this perception is inaccurate. According to Scott Thumma and Warren Bird, only 6 percent of megachurch attendees had never attended church before—only slightly better than the average of all churches in America, at 5 percent.[7] According to Mark Chaves, most megachurch growth comes not because churches have tapped into an unchurched population. Rather, it occurs "mainly because people are shifting from smaller to larger churches, not because people are shifting from uninvolvement to involvement in big churches."[8] Thumma and Bird indicate that 44 percent of megachurch attendees came from another local church, while another 28 percent came from a church farther away. Thus, 72 percent of megachurch attendees comes from other churches. Megachurches are somewhat akin to Walmart or Barnes and Noble, whose success comes at the cost of smaller businesses.[9]

Megachurches typically have three key elements that intertwine and reinforce each other. First, there is megachurch culture, which tends to be theologically light and relationally superficial, focusing more on what the church can offer than making demands of those who attend. It also tends to be consumerist, celebrity driven, and entertainment based. Second, megachurches have been among the first to employ multisite platforms that include video preaching to replicate the ministry of the pastor to other congregations *in absentia*. Third, many megachurch pastors tend to be charismatic individuals who shape their churches through their exuberant personalities and business-style leadership. They tend to be theologically undereducated, relying heavily on rhetorical skills and media savvy to woo their hearers. These three elements are not true of every megachurch, but they are common enough to formulate stereotypical views. And these elements are further reinforced as celebrity pastors are celebrated by celebrity-adoring churches, which extend their platforms beyond the church, which in turn grows pastor celebrity. And so it goes.

MEGACHURCH CULTURE

While this chapter focuses primarily on the negative aspects of megachurches, some positive aspects are worth acknowledging. According to the Hartford Institute of Religion Research's report "Megachurch 2020," megachurches, because of their greater resources of space, volunteers, and talent, are able to address special needs on a scale that most smaller churches cannot.[10] Some megachurches, like Willow Creek, have extensive ministries to the urban poor and the incarcerated.[11] Though megachurches are still predominantly white (72 percent), they are increasingly becoming multiracial.[12] And while a few megachurches have gained national attention for their political engagement, most megachurches exhibit little overt political action. They are not monolithic voting blocks, yet they report little internal conflict over political issues, probably because they wisely avoid discussing politics.[13]

Despite all the good they are able to accomplish, there remain some troubling problems at the heart of megachurch culture, philosophy, and structure. And many of these are exemplified by the massively influential megachurch of the 1980s and '90s, Willow Creek Community Church, located in the suburbs of Chicago, Illinois.

Willow Creek

"Reminiscent of a Disney park, with auditorium, huge car parks, shuttle buses, overhead screens, amazing sound systems and slick management of crowds,"[14] Willow Creek was born of the youth group of South Park Church in the Chicago suburb of Park Ridge. Bill Hybels began leading the youth group in 1972 and established its mission to reach out to unbelieving youth. The group tripled in size within a year and by 1975 had grown to a thousand members.[15] This led to the planting of a new church under Hybels' leadership, which shared the same mission, but for adults. Hybels made it the church's priority to reach out to unchurched people rather than "dig down" with current members.

The leadership team of the new church came from the original youth group led by Hybels so that its DNA would permeate Willow Creek. But because Hybels had little theological education and the church leadership came from the youth group, an "unintended consequence was virtually guaranteed: the spiritual maturity of any new leaders would likely not rise above the level of the current leadership."[16] Over the years, most of Willow Creek's ministry remained under the purview of those who were a part of that original youth group. As such, even when Willow became much bigger and older, "it remain[ed] essentially, in methodology and content, a youth group." Even its own staff have been known to refer to it as "youth ministry for big people."[17] The youth-group spirit of Willow Creek led to an intentional focus on entertainment and infotainment at the center of its methodology.

At Willow Creek's annual leadership summit fifteen years ago, Hybels himself acknowledged that the church's philosophy of ministry had been a mistake. This came after the publication of a book called *Reveal: Where Are You?* written by Greg Hawkins and Callie Parkinson, both leaders at Willow Creek. The book pointed to the failure of churches, including Willow, at the task of developing mature disciples. Hybels acknowledged that the church should have taught people how to read their own Bibles and engage spiritual practices between Sundays.[18] He acknowledged that they needed to be spiritual self-starters rather than being dependent on Sunday services for their spiritual nourishment. But by that time, Willow Creek had long been the most influential church in America, and its methodology and core principles had already been replicated by countless other churches, especially other megachurches.

Harvest Bible Chapel

Many American megachurches have been influenced by or directly modeled on Willow Creek, adopting its methodology, philosophy, and culture. But megachurches are also susceptible to other common problems because of a structure that elevates one man over the rest to the point of his becoming virtually unassailable.

Matt Stowell served more than ten years as a leader at Harvest Bible Chapel in the Chicago suburb of Rolling Meadows. Though he felt he could not raise an alarm at the time, he now acknowledges the toxic environment in which he worked. He says, "I eventually found it increasingly difficult to reconcile the person who James [McDonald] was on the stage and the James I came to know in real life."[19] Offstage, Stowell regularly witnessed McDonald's "brutal outbursts of anger, an incessant need to 'win' at all costs, berating and belittling people, cruelly joking about others, and deceptively spinning truth for his own gain."[20] While the character flaws of Harvest's celebrity preacher were a major problem in their own right, the culture of the church became shaped by the principle that "only one voice really matters." This culture meant that fear was the daily reality "more than love, or humility, or any of the other fruits of the Spirit."[21] Such fear arose from anxiety over disappointing James or being perceived to cross him in any way. Stowell describes a "culture of unholy pragmatism" at Harvest, in which staff rationalized all the ungodly offstage behavior they witnessed. They pointed to what God was doing: seats were being filled, people were being baptized, lives were being changed, and James was a gifted preacher.[22] The culture at Harvest was one in which the results were the highest value.

Former Harvest Bible Chapel elder Dan George was a member of the church for more than twenty-three years. He has since sought forgiveness for his role in perpetuating the toxic culture that protected wayward pastor James McDonald.[23] George apologized for "not listening to those who tried to bring issues to light," "for vilifying people outside Harvest who tried to bring issues to light," "for agreeing to place three of my fellow elders . . . under church discipline and excommunicating them in 2013 when they raised concerns," and "for signing a statement of 'unconditional support' for our former senior pastor."[24] George also apologized for not keeping James McDonald accountable for his actions and for supporting a structure that permitted such lack of accountability. George hopes for the deconstruction of "the old Harvest culture" and for "a new, open, honest, gracious, forgiving, loving culture" in the days ahead.[25]

Of course, not all megachurches have toxic cultures. And not all megachurch pastors are so brazenly unfit for service. But what happened at Harvest Bible Chapel should stand as a warning. The type of people elevated by megachurch culture tend to be those who are prone to abuse the culture and structure to protect their stardom, power, and personality cult. In their study of megachurch myths, even Thumma and Travis's chapter addressing the "myth" that "Megachurches Are Cults of Personality" does little to debunk that myth. They state, "The dynamics of megachurch leadership increase the possibility that the senior pastor will develop a large group of ardent admirers and followers. These devoted members can become overzealous in the amount of attention and trust they have for the senior pastor. Such a situation can develop into a cult of personality around the pastor, if not guarded against."[26]

MEGAPROBLEMS

Willow Creek and Harvest Bible Chapel are two Chicago-area megachurches that have faced some major problems and now face uncertain futures. But their wider influence, especially that of Willow, has led to similar characteristic flaws in many other megachurches as well. Regardless of how good the pastor is, how faithful the leadership is, and how sincere the attendees are, megachurch structure, philosophy, and culture tend to create unhealthy results.

Consumer Mentality

Commenting on the attitude of many megachurch-goers, David Kinnaman, vice president of Barna Research, says, "People are looking at churches with a similar cost-benefit analysis they'd give to any other consumer purchase. . . . There is little brand loyalty. Many are looking for the newest and the greatest."[27] Kinnaman is referring to consumers choosing not to sustain local businesses if they can get a better deal at a huge chain store. As Cartledge et al. ask, "Why attend the small local outlet with a fraction of the services when you can have the real thing on the other side of town? Of course, with the travel mentality of the consumer, this religious option not only affects similar churches in the same city or town but also the wider neighbouring towns and cities."[28] Megachurches tend to adapt to this consumer mindset rather than challenge it. Consequently, their seats are populated by consumers, and the most successful megachurches offer exactly what the consumers want.

Megachurches have also been likened to minimalls, one-stop shopping for everything a consumer could need. While there is some validity to this analogy, in her doctoral dissertation on megachurches, Jennifer Eaton Dyer suggests that a better analogy would be the theater. There is, of course, an economic element in the theater, since "people pay to enter a theater whether it is a movie, independent film, concert, play, or poetry reading. They 'choose' to come, and they 'spend' their time and money."[29] But a greater strength of the theater analogy is how it explains the content or "performance" that consumers encounter at megachurches. "There are actors who change their 'scripts,' a director who creates an environment for creative-restrictive play, and an audience who engages empathically with the production to be changed by the experience."[30]

The theater analogy also captures how megachurch performances affect their audiences. "Within the realm of the theater as religion, we *do* create communities of memory, experience the mystical, touch the divine, observe the sacred, worship the holy and treasure the narratives of our very existence."[31]

This latter insight articulates well the aesthetic power of the megachurch experience. For many, megachurch worship facilitates a transcendent escape from the mundanity of everyday life and, it is perceived, puts worshipers in closer touch with God. Whether or not such transcendent experiences are legitimately God ordained (it is beyond our ability to assess that question), churchgoers nevertheless behave like consumers because they seek what the megachurch experience can offer them, just as theatergoers are consumers of the experiences that the theater offers. Of course, a consumer mentality is not unique to megachurches, since smaller churches are often full of consumers too. But the particular strength of megachurches is that they provide a better product for those who seek it, and they appeal to consumerist desires. They are just more successful at shaping their product and attracting the greatest concentration of consumers.

The theatrical nature of the megachurch aesthetic is captured well by Laura Barringer's experience of visiting a church she describes as "Celebrity Central": "All the people on stage seemed to be adored by the people sitting in the seats. . . . As the service progressed, I was struck by the number of times the congregation applauded the people on stage. Without exaggeration, it was at least ten times. What occurred to me was that whenever something good was said about the church, the people applauded—which became, in essence, *self*-applause."[32]

Social Isolation from the Wider Community

Because the megachurch parallels the minimall in its ability to meet all the consumer's needs in one place, it can also induce a degree of social isolation from the wider community. According to Bill J. Leonard, dean and professor of church history at Wake Forest University, "Congregants may be able to isolate themselves from the greater community—to engage in a kind of 'Christian cocooning.'"[33] Likewise, Scott Thumma, a sociologist of religion at the Hartford Institute, says that megachurches are becoming "a parallel universe that's Christianized."[34] And Wade Clark Roof, professor of religion and society at the University of California at Santa Barbara, describes the megachurch as "the religious version of the gated community. . . . It's an attempt to create a world where you're dealing with like-minded people. . . . You lose the dialogue with the larger culture."[35] By losing dialogue with the larger culture, megachurch communities can easily form their own subcultures and become "a kind of microcosmic society, or enclave group, within which there [is] a particular set of rules, or doctrines, or dogmas which dictate the accepted system of beliefs for the worldview of the church."[36]

But such microcosms are not entirely cut off from the

wider culture and draw on certain features of it. While reacting against secular culture in general, megachurches assimilate certain aspects of it. A phenomenon known as "selectivity" is "the process of a group to choose that which they want to embrace of modernity and reject other aspects of the same culture."[37] All churches engage in this process of selectivity to some extent. The crucial question, however, is which features of secular culture can helpfully be embraced by churches. Megachurches tend to embrace the features of celebrity, consumerism, and mass-appeal entertainment.

Sucking Other Churches Dry

As we saw earlier, statistics reveal that megachurches are not especially effective in reaching the unchurched and that most of their numbers come from other churches. But statistics are abstract. In a letter to Julie Roys of *The Roys Report*, former pastor and Bible translator Paul Lundquist shares his experience. "After missionary work in Colombia with Wycliffe I pastored two Chicago-area dying churches that ultimately failed. Many pastors here can tell you that, broadly speaking, when people left our churches in the 1990s they went to Willow Creek, and when they left in the 2000s they went to Harvest Bible Chapel (or to one those churches' satellites). In smaller churches these people taught Sunday school or played the piano or served as deacons, but at Willow Creek and Harvest they typically sat in the audience and watched the show."[38]

Lundquist's experience matches that of countless other pastors who've lost scores of committed church members who stopped serving others to become recipients of megachurch Christo-entertainment.

MEGACHURCH MULTISITES

In recent years, a new trend has taken megachurch culture by storm: the multisite structure. "A multisite church is commonly defined as 'one church meeting in multiple locations.'"[39] Multisites typically rely on video preaching so that the same preacher and sermon can be heard in multiple locations at once. While the multisite structure is not entirely new, its popularity has recently skyrocketed. In the 1980s there were well under one hundred multisite churches in America; by 2012 there were eight thousand. Nearly two-thirds of megachurches are multisite, and the larger the church, the more likely it is to be multisite.[40] According to Chicago-area pastor David Jones, whose doctoral research focused on multisite video preaching, more than five million people attend multisite churches each weekend in the United States.[41]

Jones explains how multisite churches use video preaching: "Services with video preaching are called 'video venues.' A video venue is a church service like any other service. It typically features live worship. A campus pastor is on hand to shepherd those who attend. The primary difference is that the preaching pastor is not physically present, but rather preaches by video. Thus, in multisite video venues, the preaching and shepherding functions are divided between two people rather than combined in one, as in the traditional pastoral model."[42]

In the late 1990s, North Coast Church outside San Diego was multiplying services to accommodate growth. The pastor, Larry Osborne, was preaching four times each weekend and for health reasons could not do more. Rather than adding another live preaching service, the church decided to experiment with a video venue instead.[43] Three years later, 2,300 people at North Coast Church were attending video venues. Today, the church has five campuses and thirty-two services. Only four of those have in-person preaching.[44]

Jones's research on video preaching was conducted at his own church, Village Church of Barrington, which was also my home church at the time. The church had one video service and three live preaching services each weekend.

His research yielded the following conclusions:

- Those who attended the video venue were more than twice as likely to use a mobile device during the sermon to access unrelated content. (Age was not a factor in this statistic.)[45]
- Video-service attendees were four times as likely to get up from their seats and move around during the sermon.[46]
- Those who attended the video venue on a regular basis did not feel known by the preacher to the same degree as those who attended live preaching services.[47]
- There was a significantly higher percentage of lateness at the video venue.[48]
- Video-venue attendees were less likely to contribute financially to the church than those who attended live services.[49]
- Video-venue attendees reported a 56 percent decrease in motivation compared with live service attendees, and they were 12 percent less likely to apply the sermon to their lives.[50]
- Compared with those who attended only video services, those who attended live-preaching services showed a higher level of participation in fellowship, midweek ministries, and evangelism and had better attendance.[51]

For these reasons and more, Jones exhorts pastors to consider "the latent dysfunctions" of video preaching: "Those who watch may learn less, be less motivated, pay less attention, and be less involved in the church. In other words, the medium of video may have a negative effect on discipleship, especially with repeated exposure over time."[52]

Jones adds his voice to a host of evangelical critics of the multisite phenomenon, such as Thabiti Anyabwile, who describes it as an idolatrous "cult of personality multiplied and digitized for a consumer audience."[53] Parachurch ministry 9Marks, which is devoted to equipping church leaders with a biblical vision for building healthy churches,[54] published an issue of the *9Marks Journal* addressing the question of multisite churches.[55] The issue includes articles written in defense of multisite churches by theologian Gregg Allison and Baptist pastor J. D. Greear. It also includes articles critiquing the phenomenon from exegetical, theological, historical, and principled perspectives. While the issue seeks a balance of perspectives, it concludes negatively. Jonathan Leeman's article "The Alternative: Why Don't We Plant?" advocates church planting instead of adding video venues to an existing church.[56] He argues that the only reasons not to plant a church are that the church has failed to raise up other preachers or that it has decided "to accommodate celebrity and consumeristic culture."[57]

The multisite video-preaching structure seems only to enhance the problems inherent to megachurches. It further exacerbates the consumerist instinct that pervades megachurch culture, and it underscores the veneration of celebrity preachers. It is an even less effective vehicle for education and transformation. It widens the already yawning gap between preachers and their hearers. And it further dilutes megachurches' ability to disciple their constituents.

A better solution is the "multichurch" concept advanced by Brad House and Gregg Allison. Aware of the weaknesses of the video-preaching multisite model, House and Allison propose a new but related concept: multichurch is "one church expressed in multiple *churches*,"[58] which is empowered by "multiple leaders and congregations working together."[59] In case that's not clear, "a multichurch is a local community of maturing Christians who multiply their influence by launching, developing, and resourcing multiple congregations to reach its city with the gospel of Jesus Christ."[60] In other words, it's a denomination.

MEGACHURCH PASTORS

The third major factor shaping the megachurch phenomenon is the megachurch pastor. A megachurch pastor's character, gifts, and personality powerfully shape the megachurch because of the way megachurch structure elevates him to center stage.

Pastor Profile

According to Thumma, megachurches are usually the product of "one highly gifted spiritual leader."[61] Most megachurches were founded by and achieved mega status during the tenure of a single pastor, whose vision and personality shaped the character of the church. Megachurch pastors are unusually charismatic, exceptionally gifted, usually white men of an average age of fifty-three.[62] Thumma describes megachurch pastors as "visionaries and innovative spiritual entrepreneurs." They are not

161

necessarily spiritual giants, full of wisdom and insight. But they *are* entrepreneurs.

Considering their massive influence, it is concerning that less than half of megachurch pastors have earned a master of divinity degree (MDiv), which is the standard seminary training for prospective pastors.[63] More alarming, at least a third have had no seminary education at all. For example, Bill Hybels, founder and pastor of Willow Creek Church, which was the biggest church in America for several years, had no seminary training.[64] Since the numerical success of megachurches is often understood as reflecting God's blessing, megachurch pastors' relative lack of theological training is taken as a sign that theological education is not necessary and perhaps not even beneficial. There is a perception that seminary training creates stuffy pastors who know how to write an essay but don't know how to grow a church. And when the majority of "very successful" pastors don't have an MDiv, it is understandable why some would-be pastors might be skeptical about theological training.

But there are several problems with this attitude. First is the premise that numerical success is a reflection of God's blessing. It might be, but history knows plenty of cults, heresies, and murderous totalitarian regimes that were "blessed" with numerical success. I'm sure we would not want to equate such successes with God's blessing. Second, numerical success does not necessarily indicate spiritual health. Churches are not businesses that measure success purely by growth, popularity, and money. Or at least they're not supposed to be. As we'll explore, Jesus and the New Testament set very different standards that should characterize the church. Numerical size does not even come into it.

There is a certain irony that many megachurch pastors are not properly trained theologically. Since the megachurch model prioritizes the celebrity preacher's teaching to thousands and usually delegates other forms of ministry to other people, the theological quality, depth, and accuracy of his or her preaching ought to be a high priority. And while no self-respecting preacher would candidly downplay the importance of theology, many megachurch pastors do in effect downplay it by putting confidence in other factors.

Megachurch pastors are, to some extent, performers who rely on rhetorical skills, charisma, and stand-up comedy to engage, captivate, and enthrall their audiences. While content is important, of course, it tends to take a back seat to these other crowd-winning characteristics. It is certainly true that an engaging speaker has a greater ability to convey content to his hearers, but this fact should not be used to minimize the importance of the content. If anything, an engaging speaker has an even greater burden to share good content on the grounds that their content will be consumed more deeply and widely than that of less engaging preachers. An engaging speaker's theological acumen is very important. Their handling of the Scriptures is very important. Their communication of truth is very important. Megachurch pastors should never rely on their ability to entertain a crowd as a substitute for robust, learned, orthodox theology.

Unfortunately, and also ironically, the numerical success of megachurches is mistakenly understood as God's blessing by both pastor and congregation largely because the pastor does not properly teach biblical and spiritual truth to his hearers. Because he is theologically underequipped, so too are those under his theological leadership.

163

Pastor Perks, Profit, and Promotion

Esquire magazine was one of the first to report on the popular Instagram account PreachersNSneakers. The account features posts of megachurch pastors such as Carl Lentz of Hillsong, Steven Furtick of Elevation Church, Chad Veach of Zoe Church, and Levi Lusko of FreshLife Church wearing very expensive high-end sneakers and designer clothes.[65] In the *Esquire* piece "WWJD: The Ethical Conundrum of Mega-church Preachers in Super-Expensive Sneakers," Scott Christian asks, "Is it right for someone who (a) draws at least partial salary from tithing (i.e. monetary donations to the church), (b) ostensibly ministers to people who can't afford high-end swag, and (c) practices a religion whose founder was famously poor, to wear a $900 pair of Shattered Backboard Jordans while on the pulpit?"

Now with 264,000 followers at the time of this writing, the PreachersNSneakers Instagram account has clearly hit a nerve. There is something obscene about preachers displaying such levels of ostentation while many in their congregations struggle to pay the rent.

It's never good when an article begins with the sentence, "The pastors at scandalized Hillsong Church were anything but humble servants." But that's the opening salvo of the *New York Post* piece "Tithe Money Funded Hillsong Pastors' Luxury Lifestyles,"[66] published in January 2021. According to ex-congregants and staff, many pastors at Hillsong NYC used tithe-funded expense cards to pay for fancy restaurant meals, designer clothes, Kent Avenue Williamsburg high-rise living, and ATVs to zip around the neighborhood. And while Hillsong pastors lived it up on these expense cards, the church benefited from thousands of hours of volunteer labor by church members, who also paid for the pastors' expenses through their tithes. So former member Jenna Babbitt reflects, "The exploitation of free labor while these pastors are making bank is just crazy to me."

The tithes of faithful churchgoers can be used to enhance the lives of megachurch pastors in other ways too. In March 2014, *World* magazine published the piece "Unreal Sales for Driscoll's *Real Marriage*," revealing that Seattle megachurch Mars Hill "paid a California-based marketing company at least $210,000 in 2011 and 2012 to ensure that *Real Marriage*, a book written by Mark Driscoll, the church's founding pastor, and his wife, Grace, made the *New York Times* bestseller list."[67] The marketing company, ResultSource, coordinated "a nationwide network of book buyers who would purchase *Real Marriage* at locations likely to generate reportable sales for bestseller lists." Mars Hill paid for eleven thousand books, while a further six thousand books were to be purchased by individuals connected to the church. A further five thousand books were bought in bulk. The plan was successful, with *Real Marriage* spending one week on the *New York Times* bestseller list. Though the profits from the ResultSource marketing campaign went back to the church,[68] Driscoll no doubt profited from the deceitful strategy by elevating his personal profile and that of his book. A neat side-hustle alongside his $600,000 salary. *Forbes* reports that other megachurch pastors, such as Steven Furtick and Perry Noble, have also been accused of using their congregations to fund bestseller campaigns.[69]

Most megachurch pastors start out with the best of intentions. They want to serve God's people, proclaim Jesus, and do good. But they are usually gifted in a way that attracts a lot of attention to themselves, even if they don't seek it at first. After a while, celebrity and adoration go to your head. People treat you differently. The spotlight becomes addictive. Slowly, perhaps imperceptibly, these well-intentioned gifted servants become less well-intentioned. Perhaps they see the perks of their celebrity as God's blessing for a job well done, or perhaps they just develop a stronger taste for rewards now in this life. Either way, megachurch stardom is not good for their spiritual health. While many pastors remain faithful and do the best they can, many inevitably fall. Given the spiritual dangers of the megachurch structure, it's a miracle they don't all fall.

THE GOOD SHEPHERD

In John's Gospel, Jesus calls himself "the good shepherd" (John 10:11, 14). As Jesus explains, "The good shepherd lays down his life for the sheep" (v. 11); "I know my sheep and my sheep know me" (v. 14). According to Jesus, a good shepherd offers sacrificial commitment and love to the sheep. This also requires personal knowledge of the sheep—in both directions: the shepherd knows the sheep, and the sheep know the shepherd.

Shepherd imagery pervades the Bible to communicate God's intimate, courageous, sacrificial, and protective care for his people (Isaiah 40:11; Ezekiel 34:11–24; Psalm 23). In describing himself as the good shepherd, Jesus clearly identifies with this rugged role of God toward his people.[70] But he does not limit it to himself. He commissions Peter to shepherd his sheep (John 21:15–17), and Peter in turn commissions fellow church elders to "be shepherds of God's flock that is under your care, watching over them" (1 Peter 5:2). It is clearly still God's flock that elders are to watch over (not their own flocks) and that they serve under "the Chief Shepherd," Jesus (v. 4). It is worth citing Peter's full instructions to these undershepherds: "Be shepherds of God's flock that is under your care, watching over them—not because you must, but because you are willing, as God wants you to be; not pursuing dishonest gain, but eager to serve; not lording it over those entrusted to you, but being examples to the flock. And when the Chief Shepherd appears, you will receive the crown of glory that will never fade away" (vv. 2–4).

It may be God's flock, but undershepherds bear responsibility for those under their care. They are to watch over them willingly. Undershepherds are not to pursue dishonest gain. They are not to lord it over those entrusted to them. They are to be good examples. Their glory is not of this world but will be shared with them when the Chief Shepherd, Jesus, comes again.

Peter's expectations for undershepherds read like the antithesis of what we've come to expect of megachurch pastors. Of course it's not true of all, but the stereotypical megachurch pastor does not watch over God's flock with care. How can he, with two thousand people or more entrusted to him?

Too many megachurch pastors have gained notoriety for their dishonest gain, from propping up book sales via their congregations to manipulating their congregations into buying private jets for them.

There is a trend among megachurch pastors to lord it over their people through bullying, manipulation, and arrogance. Their powerful personalities often lack humility and charity. They do not tolerate dissension.

Too many megachurch pastors fail to be good examples to the flock. Because they are stars of a celebrity culture, no amount of self-deprecating false humility will undo the subliminal message that the spotlight is where God's blessing is found. Because they live in megamansions and get around in private jets, no amount of special pleading will convince us that their reward is in the next life or that true greatness is found through serving others (Mark 10:43).

There are many exceptions to this stereotype, of course. There are hundreds, if not thousands, of megachurch pastors we never hear about because they've avoided scandal and mass celebrity. But the megachurch pastors who *are* known to us because of scandal or mass celebrity (often both) raise a legitimate question: just how healthy is the megachurch model *for pastors*? It's obviously not very healthy for many of those who attend, but we don't often reflect on how it affects the stars of the show. Is there something intrinsically unhealthy about this structure that overburdens leaders with opportunities leading them to corruption? They are only human, after all. If you offer fame, money, adoration, and power to almost anyone, they will eventually spoil.

A chief problem with the megachurch model is that it makes it very difficult for a pastor to be a good shepherd. He cannot know his flock and they cannot know him—at least, not well enough. He can run an organization, but he cannot watch over his flock, and it is difficult to be an example to those who do not really know him. The megachurch pastor will also struggle to live for next-worldly glory when there is the temptation to experience stardom now. Any pastor will fail to be a faithful undershepherd while *he* is the star of the show, rather than the Chief Shepherd, Jesus.

Likewise, the megachurch model makes it difficult for its members to be a good flock. The sheer size of megachurch congregations invites anonymity, spectatorship, consumerism, and lack of meaningful engagement beyond the Sunday show. Lacking a shepherd-pastor, the congregation will be like sheep without a shepherd.

If a clever wolf wanted to destroy God's flock, the following four-step strategy would do the trick. Step one: take the sheep away from the good shepherds leading small churches and put them all under a bad shepherd in one big church. Step two: wait for the good shepherds' small churches to close. Step three: let the bad shepherd lead the flock astray through weak teaching and self-centered consumerism. Step four: let the bad shepherd fall when his true nature becomes known. The result? All the good small churches are gone. The good shepherds have left the ministry. Their former flocks have become corrupted. And the big church juggernaut is no longer able to function without its celebrity bad shepherd. It would be a devastating strategy.

JESUS THE BODYBUILDER

An Anglican church in Sydney has an interesting stained-glass window. It depicts the postresurrection Jesus, who is muscular with ripped abs. When I saw it, I thought, well, the Gospels don't describe Jesus in such a way, but then, they don't describe his physique at all, before or after his resurrection. The New Testament does regard Jesus' resurrected body as one of glory, having been transfigured in some sense (1 Corinthians 15:42–49), so I guess this artist decided that probably involved a cut midsection.

Jesus *is* a bodybuilder. But not in that sense. The body he builds is his church. According to Paul, "Christ himself gave the apostles, the prophets, the evangelists, the pastors and teachers, to equip his people for works of service, so that the body of Christ may be built up until we all reach unity in the faith in the knowledge of the Son of God and become mature, attaining to the whole measure of the fullness of Christ" (Ephesians 4:11–13).

Christ gave servants such as apostles and prophets so that his body would be built up. Notice that pastors and teachers are among this group of servants. The way they are described in the original language implies that they are pastor-teachers, not two roles fulfilled by two people (a pastor and a teacher) but two roles embodied in a single person—a pastor-teacher. Or, according to biblical scholar Harold Hoehner, "it could be said that all pastors should be teachers but not all teachers are pastors."[71] The megachurch pastor, however, is rarely able to be a pastor-teacher. He will be a teacher of thousands, even of those not in his physical presence, but cannot possibly be a pastor-teacher because he cannot pastor thousands of people (especially those he does not even see in person). The megachurch model bifurcates the pastor-teacher role into two roles so that the celebrity preacher does the teaching while other members of his team do the pastoring. But since the main teaching is left to the celebrity preacher, these other pastors often do not teach; hence they are not pastor-teachers either. As a result, megachurches might be left without a pastor-teacher at all.

Notice also that the pastor-teachers, along with the other servants, such as apostles and prophets, are not the ones who do the bodybuilding. No, they are "to equip his people for works of service, so that the body of Christ may be built up" (v. 12). They are *to equip* Jesus' people to do the bodybuilding. As we've seen, a huge problem with the megachurch model is that it reinforces a consumerist attitude toward church. The celebrity preacher, the worship team, and whoever else is onstage put on the show while everyone else passively takes it in. The church receives ministry, but it does not *do* the ministry. That's what the paid staff of the church are for. But according to Paul, the staff of the church are to help the people to serve, not to do all the ministry themselves. The failure to do so is not unique to megachurches, of course. Small churches may also overprofessionalize ministry so that it is the purview of the employed staff rather than the responsibility of the whole congregation. But megachurches exacerbate this problem through their scale and size. Their theaterlike experience communicates that ministry is to be consumed rather than shared.

Some may argue that megachurches are great for bodybuilding, since they get so huge. But this assumes that Christ's bodybuilding is all about size. According to Ephesians 4, it has nothing to do with size, which isn't even mentioned. Rather, the body will be built up "until we all reach unity in the faith and in the knowledge of the Son of God and become mature, attaining to the whole measure of the fullness of Christ" (v. 13). Bodybuilding is about the maturity of the body, not its size. Maturity is seen in its "unity in the faith," in its "knowledge of the Son of God," and in its reaching "the fullness of Christ." Since very large congregations are weak in developing the maturity of believers' faith, they are therefore weak bodybuilders.

The effects of Christ's bodybuilding are spelled out further in the following verses: "Then we will no longer be infants, tossed back and forth by the waves, and blown here and there by every wind of teaching and by the cunning and craftiness of people in their deceitful scheming. Instead, speaking the truth in love, we will grow to become in every respect the mature body of him who is the head, that is, Christ. From him the whole body, joined and held together by every supporting ligament, grows and builds itself up in love, as each part does its work" (vv. 14–16).

Maturity includes the ability to discern good teaching from bad (v. 14). Maturity involves speaking the truth to one another in love (v. 15). Maturity includes becoming a body fit for its head, Christ (v. 15). This body "builds itself up in love, as each part does its work" (v. 16).

Megachurches do not facilitate speaking the truth to one another, since most people do not know most other people there. And megachurches do not enable the body to build itself up in love, because the church consumes rather than builds and because they do not know each other in order to love. Each part does not do its work because only 2 percent of the church does anything.

If bodybuilding were all about size, megachurches would be the Arnold Schwarzeneggers of Christianity. But Christ's bodybuilding is about quality and maturity, not size. In Arnold's heyday, his huge size was all muscle. You could get bigger than him if you got really, really fat, but that would miss the point of bodybuilding. So, too, megachurches often miss the point. It's not about size. It's about quality. David Wells comments, "It is very easy to build churches in which seekers congregate; it is very hard to build churches in which biblical faith is maturing into genuine discipleship."[72] Megachurches have way too much fat and not enough muscle.

Since megachurches robbed Paul Lundquist of the churches under his care, I thought I'd let him have the last word on the subject. "A church is a gathering of God's people in Christ, not a stadium with a star celebrity whose gifts and charisma attract a crowd. Megachurches of this model are seedbeds of spiritual corruption. Flee them. . . . *All* multisite megachurches are spiritual Chernobyls. Evangelicalism is redeemable but megachurches are not. Run away. Attend a church where some humble, unassuming servant of God preaches verse-by-verse through the pages of Holy Scripture."[73]

MARKS OF A HEALTHY CHURCH

A highlight of my years living in the States was my annual visit to Capitol Hill Baptist Church (CHBC) in Washington, DC. Each visit of three or four days over a weekend gave me the opportunity to hang out with my friend senior-pastor Mark Dever and to preach at the Sunday morning service. And on each visit I was struck by several characteristics of the church. First it should be noted that Mark is a big deal in conservative evangelical circles. He's a founding member of Together for the Gospel (T4G), was on the council of the Gospel Coalition (TGC), and is the founder and president of 9Marks ministries, which serves thousands of church leaders. With a doctorate in church history from Cambridge, he has written more than twenty books and is invited to speak around the world. Considering his celebrity, many would assume that CHBC is a megachurch. But it's not. Why not? Because, as Mark says, their building seats a thousand people. And since that's the building God has given them, that's the maximum size of the church. They don't believe in multiple services, and certainly not multisites. When mature Christians move to town and visit CHBC, they're warmly welcomed and then encouraged to join one of the other good churches in the city that could use their help. The worship is not showy and frequently includes old hymns with great lyrics. Sermons regularly reach an hour or more in length and consist of rigorous explanation of the text. Mark stands at the door after each Sunday service and greets everyone as they leave. I'm always struck by how he seems to know everyone and how everyone has such evident affection for him. His study (on the first floor of his home) is open to anyone who wants to drop in—at any time. People just hang out there and Mark chats with them as he writes his sermons. CHBC's intern program welcomes dozens of pastors-in-training each year, who spend six months with the church, receiving input from Mark and his team, and then are sent off to serve in other churches. Many of the long-term staff are eventually sent out to pastor other churches too. CHBC could easily become a megachurch, but their focus is not on size. It's on maturity. It's on loving relationships. And it's on meeting Jesus in his Word.

EIGHT

THE LUNATIC FRINGE

Many will say to me on that day, "Lord, Lord, did
we not prophesy in your name and in your name
drive out demons and in your name perform many
miracles?" Then I will tell them plainly, "I never
knew you. Away from me, you evildoers!"

SOME OF THE EVANGELICALS WHO MAKE THE NEWS SEEM TO
know little of the Bible and distort its teachings. They would
not be recognized as evangelicals by most who have had that
label within the five-hundred-year history of the movement. Yet
they embrace the label, perhaps for legitimization or political
purposes, providing further evidence that the term *evangelical* is
dying or is already dead.

We might define *theological evangelicals* as those who share
certain historic evangelical beliefs, perhaps those described by
Bebbington's quadrilateral of conversionism, activism, biblicism,
and crucicentrism.[1] But the meaning of the term is seriously

compromised when leaders such as Paula White, Kenneth Copeland, and Joel Osteen are identified as evangelicals too. Few theological evangelicals would recognize such people as fellow evangelicals. While referring to them as the lunatic fringe might seem a bit severe, it expresses what many evangelicals think, even if they're too polite to say so.

If the lunatic fringe remained on the fringe, it would not be such a problem for evangelicalism. But the massive churches, huge followings, media exposure, celebrity connections, and occasional controversies of those on the fringe give them increasingly mainstream status.[2] When society at large thinks "Paula White = evangelical," we know the definition of *evangelical* has changed. By way of analogy, a similar thing has happened to non-Trump Republicans. The Republican label has been supplanted by a movement that does not represent many of the values traditionally associated with the Republican Party. Non-Trump Republicans feel increasingly alienated within their own party even now that Trump has left office. There comes a point at which *Republican* no longer means what it once meant; the meaning of the term has shifted. Traditional Republicans might feel ashamed of the label when it is now associated so closely with Donald Trump and everything he represents, to the point where former officials imagine a future split in the Republican Party so that traditional Republicans and Trump Republicans can go their separate ways.[3] It seems that evangelicalism has reached a similar crisis. Many theological evangelicals feel ashamed of the term *evangelical*, and a splitting of the movement seems inevitable.

In both of these cultures—the Republican Party and evangelicalism—a crisis of identity is perpetrated when what was formerly a fringe element takes center stage. Though the fringe element was once dismissed or ignored, it is no longer on the periphery. It redefines the center of the movement as it pulls in its adherents, reshapes the majority, and alienates its critics. So Fred Clark opines, "It's really the old-guard 'mainstream' that is now the fringe—the marginal, inconsequential, only begrudgingly accepted faction of the larger family whose presence in it is a source of embarrassment for the rest."[4] The lunatics have overrun the asylum.

ON THE FRINGE

Sadly, there are many examples of those on the fringe we can choose for review. We'll look briefly at three of the most prominent—Kenneth Copeland, Joel Osteen, and Paula White—but this group includes others like Benny Hinn, T. D. Jakes, Joyce Meyer, and Creflo Dollar, to name just a few. And the fringe is dangerous primarily because of the false gospels it promotes. Given that the fringe elements have now found their way to center stage, their kookiness, formerly overlooked or a matter of embarrassment, has precipitated a devastating redefinition of the movement.

The Prosperity Gospel

Kenneth Copeland is a televangelist based in Fort Worth, Texas, whose programs are viewed in more than 130 countries. He's worth at least $300 million and has used his ministry's tax-exempt status to fund a lavish lifestyle complete with mansions, private jets, and an airport. Answering criticisms as to why he needed an expensive private jet, Copeland replied that you can't talk to God while flying commercial. "You can't manage that today, in this dope-filled world, get in a long tube with a bunch of demons." Copeland clarified that he did not mean to say that people who travel commercially are demons, but he sort of did.[5]

Copeland has claimed that COVID-19 was caused by President Trump's opponents, who had "opened the door" for the virus through their "displays of hate" toward the president. He told his viewers that they could be healed of the virus, however, by touching their screens. Given the importance of Copeland's ministry in the face of COVID-19, he encouraged his viewers to continue giving to the ministry even if they had lost their jobs because of the pandemic. Finally, in 2020 Copeland decided to destroy COVID-19 once and for all by blowing "the wind of God" on it. He blew air at the camera and said, "I blow the wind of God on you. You are destroyed forever, and you'll never be back. Thank you, God." He declared that COVID-19 was "finished" and "over."[6] Most traditional evangelicals would agree: Copeland sure is full of wind.

Copeland is a proponent of what is referred to as the prosperity gospel, the false belief that God will make you healthy, successful, and wealthy if only you have enough faith. God's chief purpose in life is to give you everything you ever wanted, because God is happiest when you're happiest. This means that times of difficulty, suffering, or hardship are really your own fault because you do not have enough faith.

One of the chief ways that believers can express their faith is to give money to their church. That's why so many prosperity preachers emphasize the importance of giving; if you give to God, he will give back to you. Of course, believers are not really giving their hard-earned money to *God* but to the preachers who've taught them to do so. In that sense, the prosperity gospel does have a ring of truth to it—for its preachers. The more they preach prosperity, the richer they get.

It's shocking how many people fall for the prosperity gospel, which is so self-evidently false. It's shocking that people who sometimes read some of the Bible can think that God's main purpose in life is to bless you with whatever you want. It's shocking that Paula White can say, "Anyone who tells you to deny yourself is from Satan,"[7] when that's exactly what Jesus tells his followers to do (Matthew 16:24). It's shocking how little the prosperity gospel has to do with the teaching of the Bible.

An entire, and rather long, book of the Bible is dedicated to disentangling the false idea that the good and bad things that happen to us depend on how much faith we have. In the first chapter of the book, we learn that the great suffering that Job is about to endure has nothing to do with how faithful he is (Job 1:6–12). A major question of the book is whether Job will remain faithful *even though* God will allow him to experience incredible suffering.[8] Job teaches the opposite of the prosperity gospel. There is no one-to-one correspondence between our faithfulness and the good and bad things that happen to us. Of course, there are often natural consequences for our actions, good and bad, as Proverbs and common sense teach. But unprovoked suffering is not an indicator of faithlessness. It's a test of our faithfulness. Will we trust God in good times and bad?

You have to wonder what the adherents of the prosperity gospel think about the apostle Paul, who suffered terribly, was many times imprisoned, beaten, and stoned, and was finally executed, probably without a denarius to his name. Did Paul lack enough faith for God to bless him with a luxurious life? What about twelve of the thirteen apostles (including Paul as number thirteen) who all died cruel deaths for Jesus' sake?[9] Did they lack enough faith to be blessed by God? And then there's Jesus himself. He did not amass a fortune or live in luxury. He was a pauper and counseled others to give their money to the poor, yet prosperity preachers are multimillionaires and counsel others to give their money to the rich. And let's not forget that Jesus was betrayed, beaten, insulted, flogged, and then crucified, the most cruel and vicious way the Romans could dream up to execute someone. Perhaps if Jesus had had enough faith, all that wouldn't have happened to him. He could have married Mary Magdalene, bought a nice house in the suburbs, and lived a life of comfort.

Jesus warned about the spiritual dangers of greed and wealth. He said it's hard for the rich to enter the kingdom of God (Matthew 19:23), that you cannot serve both God and money (Matthew 6:24), to be on your guard against all kinds of greed (Luke 12:15), and that a person can gain the world but lose his soul (Mark 8:36). According to Ross Douthat, "This is where the union of God and Mammon goes astray, ultimately: it succumbs to a naïveté about how riches are often accumulated and about the dark pull that money can exert over the human heart."[10] Despite such warnings, the Bible does not regard wealth as inherently bad. It certainly can be a blessing from God, as the book of Proverbs regularly acknowledges. But wealth *is* dangerous because it is easy to treasure the wrong things, to depend on ourselves rather than God, and to hoard good things for ourselves while others go without. The love of money, Paul warns his ministry apprentice Timothy, is "a root of all kinds of evil" (1 Timothy 6:10).

The Bible never promises that the faithful will be rewarded with wealth and health in this life. Such things may come as the blessing of God, but they are not guaranteed, which is patently self-evident from countless godly examples in the Bible and countless more throughout history. There are simply no grounds to believe that we can strike a deal with God in which our faithfulness is rewarded with material wealth, health, and success. But the Bible does make certain promises to believers, one of which is found in Paul's words in 2 Timothy 3:12: "Everyone who wants to live a godly life in Christ Jesus will be persecuted." Are the faithful guaranteed prosperity? No. But the godly are guaranteed persecution of some sort. Persecution can safely be regarded as the opposite of prosperity. Persecution is painful, unjust, and damaging. Those who want to live a godly life in Christ Jesus are signing up for persecution, not this world's riches. They follow Jesus, who taught them to deny themselves, take up their crosses, and follow him.[11] They seek the kingdom of God, not the comforts of this world. They look forward to a future "inheritance that can never perish, spoil or fade" (1 Peter 1:4). True followers of Jesus are not in it for their prosperity. If they do happen to be blessed with material wealth, they will share it with those who need it in the spirit of generosity.

The Life-Coach Gospel

"The most influential work of popular theology published this century comes with a glossy gold dust jacket and a slew of celebrity blurbs on the back. . . . The author himself gazes out from the front cover: his black hair is piled up and slick with gel; his hands are extended and touching at the fingertips; his smile is enormous, front teeth like piano keys or filed-down tusks. The book's title hovers like an angel above his left shoulder, promising *Your Best Life Now: Seven Steps to Living at Your Full Potential.*"[12]

So reads Ross Douthat's introduction to Joel Osteen, the pastor of the biggest Protestant church in America—Lakewood Church in Houston, Texas—whose sermons are viewed by millions every week in more than a hundred countries. As of 2017, Osteen is worth around $60 million and lives in a $10.5 million home.[13] Though Osteen no longer draws a salary from Lakewood Church, the megachurch spends tens of millions of dollars every year on its television broadcasts. It's an extremely effective platform for Osteen's books and brand. He received a $13 million advance for his second book, *Become a Better You*, and has published several since.[14]

Osteen is not theologically trained and his messages are distinctly nontheological. He prefers to view himself as "a [life] coach, as a motivator to help [people] experience the life of God that God has for them."[15] Presenting himself as a self-help coach makes Osteen feel more palatable than some of the other prosperity preachers, like Kenneth Copeland and Paula White, but his message is more or less the same. He teaches that "if you do your part, God will do his. He will promote you. He'll give you increase."[16] In order for them to receive God's blessings, Osteen encourages his hearers to give beyond their means. He appeals to God's lack of hesitation in creating the universe; he didn't check with accounting to see if he could afford to create the stars, galaxies, and planets. He didn't google it to see whether it was possible, so we can achieve anything we want too.[17] Edward Luce of *Financial Times* comments that Lakewood's business model "seems like a vehicle to redistribute money upwards—towards heaven, perhaps—rather than to those who need it."[18]

And Ross Douthat suggests that Osteen embodies "the refashioning of Christianity to suit an age of abundance, in which the old war between monotheism and money seems to have ended, for many believers, in a marriage of God and Mammon."[19]

There's nothing wrong with life coaching. Coaches can offer helpful tips and tools for people to get their careers, relationships, and lives on track. Indeed, the Bible shares much wisdom designed to promote the good life. The book of Proverbs, for example, is chock full of good advice, sensible warnings, and insights into life. We would do well to live according to the "coaching" of Proverbs. The life-coach gospel, however, takes these good things and makes them the *god* thing. And that's a problem. When we turn a good thing into a god thing, we are committing idolatry. For me, playing and performing music is a lifelong passion, and I consider music a gift from God. But if I make music the god of my life (as I once did), I allow one of God's good gifts to take the place of God himself. Something becomes a god thing when we worship it and prize it above all else. But Bible 101 teaches that God alone is God and that he alone ought to be worshiped. Hence the first commandment: "Do not have other gods besides me. Do not make an idol for yourself" (Exodus 20:3–4 CSB). If the highest concern of preaching is life coaching or if the good life is the object of worship, the preacher has substituted good advice for God. And that's idolatry.

If we scratch the surface a little more, we see that life coaching has its own god thing. The self. Whenever we focus on life coaching, we are focusing on ourselves—our careers, our relationships, our lives. While there's nothing wrong with paying appropriate attention to ourselves, we're not the center of the universe. The Bible counsels us to understand ourselves as God's creatures, made by him and made for him. As we consider ourselves, therefore, we are led to consider our Creator, who has so wonderfully made us. And that in turn ought to lead us to acknowledge him with praise and thanksgiving. But life coaching sees ourselves and our well-being as the ultimate goal, rather than the praise and worship of God. According to the life-coach gospel, God is there to help us to achieve our life goals. He is the big coach in the sky who exists for our well-being. As such, the life-coach gospel promotes an anthropocentric (human centered) universe rather than a theocentric (God centered) one.

Joel Osteen seems like a nice guy and he has some good coaching tips. But with its main focus on life coaching and its absence of theology, his Lakewood Church is effectively a big self-help center. God and Jesus are sprinkled in, for sure, but they are not the center of things. Self and self-interest are. And that's the secret growth strategy of America's biggest megachurch: make it about *them* and they will come. Nothing's as appealing as self-interest.

The Nationalism Gospel

Paula White rocketed to mainstream prominence as Donald Trump's spiritual advisor and chair of his evangelical advisory board. She delivered the invocation at Trump's presidential inauguration in January 2017. White took an advisory role in the Trump administration in 2019, leaving her position as senior pastor of New Destiny Christian Center, a nondenominational megachurch in Florida.

Jeremy Peter and Elizabeth Dias wrote that White is

"an outsider whose populist brand of Christianity mirrors Mr. Trump's conquest of the Republican Party. And she is in many ways a quintessentially Trump figure: a television preacher, married three times, who lives in a mansion."[20]

Trump and White were both outsiders who "often faced suspicion and scorn from more conventional, established leaders of the spheres in which they sought acceptance."[21] In spite of mainstream opposition and financial scandal,[22] they both achieved a prominence and dominance once thought improbable.

In 2019, White led a prayer meeting with other evangelical leaders in which she prayed condemning the president's enemies, claiming they were aligned with evil spirits and employed sorcery.[23] She prayed, "Any person [or] entities that are aligned against the president will be exposed and dealt with and overturned by the superior blood of Jesus."[24] She continued, "Whether it's the spirit of Leviathan, a spirit of Jezebel, Abaddon, whether it's the spirit of Belial, we come against the strongmen, especially Jezebel, that which would operate in sorcery and witchcraft, that which would operate in hidden things, veiled things, that which would operate in deception."[25]

To help secure Trump's reelection, in 2020 White called on "angelic reinforcement" from Africa and South America. She claimed to "hear a sound of victory," since "angels have even been dispatched from Africa right now. . . . In the name of Jesus from South America, they're coming here."[26] Such angelic support was apparently necessary to counteract the "demonic confederacies . . . attempting to steal the election from Trump."[27]

We addressed the evangelical pursuit of political power in the first chapter, but the flip side of this pursuit is allowing nationalistic themes and concerns to seep into Christian faith or imposing politics on Christianity. In America, the nationalism gospel is most obvious when the spoken or unspoken rule is that evangelicals must vote Republican or they are no longer Christian. Voting Republican is not simply the preferred choice of those who would like to promote certain values dear to evangelicals, it is their *Christian* duty to vote Republican. If that sounds exaggerated, consider the opinion of evangelical superstar John MacArthur on the matter. MacArthur is on the other side of the spectrum from Paula White, who does not teach the Bible and doesn't even seem to know it. MacArthur is a serious Bible teacher, widely respected for his handling of the text and for his bona fide evangelical credentials. But even MacArthur has said that "from a biblical standpoint, Christians could not vote Democrat." He told President Trump in August 2020 that "any real, true believer is going to be on your side in this election."[28]

MacArthur is not claiming that voting Republican is a prerequisite of Christian faith, as though entry into Jesus' kingdom is based on repentance, faith, and votes. He's not saying that God will hold your voting record against you while erasing your record of sin. Rather, MacArthur, along with many evangelicals today, takes "correct" voting as a sign that someone is a true believer. A genuine believer, who believes the Bible and seeks to honor Jesus, has no choice but to vote Republican. To do otherwise is evidence that someone is not a genuine believer.

But this is a ludicrous claim. First, it confuses the interplay between faith and politics. As we argued in the first chapter, political strategies are not effective ways to promote Jesus. Hearts are not transformed by law. No one is going to follow Jesus because their desire to live a certain way is suddenly outlawed.

Such action simply alienates evangelicals even further from the wider society for all the wrong reasons.

Second, MacArthur's claim unhelpfully adopts a theocratic vision of democracy in which the rule of the people should be used to establish the rule of God. But Jesus' kingdom is not of this world. There is no democracy, monarchy, or socialist state that is God's kingdom on earth, as Israel, in the Old Testament, was once supposed to be. Christians have no business trying to overlay a theocracy on a democracy.

Third, his claim makes assumptions about which values are the "Christian" ones. According to MacArthur and others, Christians must vote Republican because that is the anti-abortion, anti-gay-marriage, and anti-trans-activism party (among other things). But Democrats are not defined by only these issues. They are also pro caring for the poor, pro welcoming the alien and stranger, pro universal health care, and pro accessible education. And they're anti guns. So how do evangelicals decide which of these issues are more Christian than the others? The Bible has a lot more to say about caring for the poor and welcoming the stranger than it does about protecting gun rights. Evangelicals like MacArthur have accepted a narrative that determines which political values are the Christian ones, and therefore which party is more Christian than the other. Voting according to the preferred party is therefore a Christian duty. But the reality is that there is no "Christian vote." Each believer must weigh up the issues, the political positions of both sides, love for their neighbors, and the character and integrity of their leaders, and then prayerfully vote according to their conscience. Christians should vote. But there is no Christian vote.

American Civil Religion

Another indicator of the nationalism gospel is the close association of Christianity and American civil religion. The *God Bless the USA Bible* is a recent example. This volume packages the US Constitution, the Bill of Rights, the Declaration of Independence, and the Pledge of Allegiance in a King James Version translation of the Bible. It is advertised as "the Ultimate American Bible."[29]

No one believes that these foundational US documents are Scripture. But Americans tend to treat them as sacred documents nonetheless. Since Christians regard the Bible as sacred Scripture, putting these two types of "sacred" texts together says something alarming. It suggests that real Americans are Christians and that the Bible is somehow pro USA, yet both suggestions are implausible. American Christians might consider how they'd feel if Muslims produced a version of the Qur'an printed with the US Constitution. Would they interpret that as a claim of some sort, either about America or about the Qur'an?

The binding of US founding documents with the Bible suggests that there is something inherently Christian about these documents. Surely, they have been influenced by biblical thought. But also they assert the importance of freedom of religion over the worship of God, contrary to the Bible. Moreover, can we say that the Bible belongs to America exclusively? Is America God's special country? Should Americans read their founding documents with the same devotion with which they read the Bible? Should those documents form part of Christians' regular Bible study? Should preachers include the founding documents in their sermons? Should non-Americans repent and believe in the Constitution?

The *God Bless the USA Bible* is just the latest example of how American civil religion influences American Christianity. In his seminal 1967 article, "Civil Religion in America,"[30] Robert Bellah compares the two: "What we have, then, from the earliest years of the republic is a collection of beliefs, symbols, and rituals with respect to sacred things and institutionalized in a collectivity. This religion—there seems no other word for it—while not antithetical to and indeed sharing much in common with Christianity, was neither sectarian nor in any specific sense Christian."[31]

American civil religion was never intended to substitute for Christianity, because each has distinct functions. Personal piety and voluntary social action are the purview of the church, while national leadership operates under the rubric of civil religion.[32] American civil religion "borrowed selectively from the religious tradition in such a way that the average American saw no conflict between the two."[33] Indeed, civil religion and the church have been able to cooperate for the creation of national solidarity, with many of civil religion's themes derived from the Bible. As Bellah explains, "Behind the civil religion at every point lie Biblical archetypes: Exodus, Chosen People, Promised Land, New Jerusalem, Sacrificial Death and Rebirth. But it is also genuinely American and genuinely new. It has its own prophets and its own martyrs, its own sacred events and sacred places, its own solemn rituals and symbols."[34]

I'm not sure there's anything inherently wrong with American civil religion. I don't see a problem with shaping a nation's identity around biblical themes and Christian ideals, or regarding a nation as blessed by God. But the problems begin when civil religion blurs with Christianity. People get into debates about whether America is a Christian nation. And, more important for our purposes, Christianity becomes misshapen by the interests of nationalism.

I can see why all of this would be confusing for American Christians. If you grow up with a civil-religious understanding of American identity with a reverence for the founding documents and an indebtedness to the themes of the Bible and Christianity, it can be difficult not to conflate the two. American civil religion pervades American culture. But when it is confused with the Christian faith, this confusion is syncretism—the blending of non-Christian religious ideas with Christian faith.

American Christians are understandably critical of syncretism in other cultures, such as African Christianity blended with ancestor worship. Ancestor worship is an inherited cultural artifact that many Africans have continued to practice alongside their relatively new Christian faith. They don't necessarily see the problem with it. But for non-Africans, ancestor worship is an obvious pollution of Christianity. The two are incompatible, and it is difficult to imagine how authentic Christian faith can be maintained alongside ancestor worship. We might say that ancestor worship is an African Christian blind spot. In the same way, the blending of American civil religion with Christianity is an American Christian blind spot. (We have our own blind spots in Australia too, but, by definition, I need others to tell me what they are.)

The syncretism of American civil religion and Christianity has led to the nationalism gospel, which is as false as the prosperity and life-coach gospels. All three false gospels do significant harm to would-be followers of Jesus. They also do great harm to the promotion of Jesus in the wider culture, which is repulsed by their greed, self-centeredness, and Ameridolatry. But just as the lunatics have left the periphery and become mainstream, so the false gospels they promote have become synonymous with American evangelicalism.

THE EVANGELICAL POPE

New York Times columnist David Brooks once wrote that if evangelicals could have elected a pope, John Stott would have been their choice.[35] In 2005, the late English Anglican cleric and theologian was ranked by *Time* as among the one hundred most influential people in the world.[36] Stott's more than fifty books have sold in the millions, and all their royalties fund Langham Partnership, a ministry that Stott founded to train and equip leaders of the Global South. A theological evangelical, Stott emphasized the authority of the Scriptures and the centrality of Jesus' death. He also championed the importance of the Christian mind and opposed anti-intellectualism. He was a dedicated evangelist *and* he was passionately committed to justice for the poor and the care of creation. Stott pioneered the renaissance of biblical expository preaching, in which the text of the Bible takes center stage as it is carefully explained and applied. Millions of evangelicals around the world have been deeply influenced by Stott's ministry and teaching.

Stott remained single his whole life and was known to friends as "Uncle John," a beloved friend and brother who exemplified deep humility alongside his astonishing gifts and leadership. He lived in a simple two-bedroom flat in London and declined countless invitations to be elevated within the Anglican Church.

Biblical scholar Christopher Wright reflects, "He was, for all of us who knew him, a walking embodiment of the simple beauty of Jesus, whom he loved above all else."[37]

Evangelicalism would be in much better shape today if the likes of John Stott occupied center stage and the lunatics remained on the fringe. This is as much for their own sakes as everyone else's, since I fear they will find themselves on the wrong end of Jesus' disturbing words in Matthew 7:22–23: "Many will say to me on that day, 'Lord, Lord, did we not prophesy in your name and in your name drive out demons and in your name perform many miracles?' Then I will tell them plainly, 'I never knew you. Away from me, you evildoers!'"

The exponents of the lunatic fringe regularly lay claim to prophecies, exorcisms, and the miraculous in Jesus' name, but there is little compelling evidence that they genuinely know Jesus. Their private jets and mansions, false prophecies, big book deals, lack of basic biblical knowledge, and blatant self-centeredness and self-promotion belie true knowledge of Jesus. On the other hand, John Stott exuded personal knowledge of Jesus by his humble, generous, unassuming, others-centered life of service. He embodied the simple beauty of Jesus. The differences between him and the lunatic fringe could not be clearer.

NINE

SAVING FAITH

For the Son of Man came to seek and to save the lost.

THOUGH I HAVE BEEN CRITICAL OF EVANGELICALISM IN THIS book, my aim, rather than disparaging Christian faith, Jesus, and the Bible, has been to uphold their dignity. By revealing various evangelical distortions, my hope is to renew wider interest in Jesus, while calling evangelicals to take note of the elements of his teaching that speak into current concerns. Though the book has taken aim at faults within evangelicalism, it does not take issue with Jesus or the Bible. As I've argued throughout, Jesus and the Bible stand against the dangerous faults within evangelicalism. For some evangelicals, this distinction will be difficult to accept. For them, evangelicalism *is* Jesus and the Bible. Jesus is the center of their faith, and the Bible is the ground of their faith. If you reject evangelicalism, they reason, you are rejecting both Jesus and the Bible. But this is false. Evangelicals do not have a monopoly on Jesus or the Bible. Jesus does not belong to them.

The first step in correcting evangelicalism's faults is to recognize this distinction between the movement and Jesus. Jesus may be the center of evangelical faith, but that does not mean that Jesus = evangelicalism = Jesus. And it does not mean that Jesus has no criticism of his own for evangelicals. Jesus sees what is true, and he disciplines those he loves, just as he critiques the churches of Asia Minor in Revelation 2–3. These were Christian churches centered on Jesus, and yet he candidly exposed their faults. If anything, Jesus' true worshipers should expect his loving course correction to prevent them from shipwrecking their faith. And evangelicals are in real danger of being dashed against the rocks if they are not willing to listen to Jesus. In this concluding chapter, we'll seek to understand the primary instincts that give rise to evangelicalism's faults. And we'll seek to address them by looking at Jesus afresh. Finally, we'll explore some final concerns related to using or adopting the evangelical label.

FOIBLES AND FAULT LINES

No one's perfect. No church is perfect. And no Christian movement is perfect. Some of evangelicalism's problems are just regular human problems. Some are not that serious. They are merely evangelical foibles—minor weaknesses or small defects that we might expect of any group or movement. It's not fair to nitpick such foibles, just as we wouldn't appreciate someone nitpicking our personal foibles. But some of evangelicalism's problems are more like fault lines than foibles. They have real destructive power that can shake the foundations of faith and swallow people whole. Pointing out such fault lines is not a danger to evangelicalism but a warning of the dangers it already faces.

Much of the ground covered in this book has necessarily simplified issues that are quite complex. But it is worth distilling even further the causes of these evangelical fault lines. The major problems we exposed in previous chapters may be summarized as follows:

- American evangelicalism has become politicized to the extent that its spiritual nature has been distorted, fueled by the assumption that political power will transform American culture.
- Evangelicals often uphold an "us versus them" mentality toward outsiders, shaped by a lack of self-sacrificial love and acceptance of others.
- Evangelicalism frequently suffers from the perception and reality of judgmentalism, forged by self-righteousness and a lack of humility.
- Evangelicals can be highly divisive, exacerbating theological and cultural divisions that create tribal boundaries established by tribal ways of reading the Bible.
- Evangelicals have an understood code of acceptable and unacceptable sins, created through tribal values rather than the priorities of the Bible.
- Evangelicals tend to shoot their wounded by the way they treat marriage failure, divorce, and remarriage.
- Evangelicals celebrate an unhealthy church model—the megachurch—which is the product of a cultural fascination with celebrity, size, consumerism, and entertainment.

195

- The popular face of evangelicalism has been overrun by fringe personalities peddling false gospels aimed at the manipulation of their followers to forge their own fortunes.

What's underneath these problems? I would suggest that evangelicals tend to value and trust in the wrong things.

Some of the things that evangelicals value but shouldn't include cultural dominance, the security that comes from tribal membership, tribal conformity, celebrity, popular success, and wealth. These values have little to do with Jesus and reflect the values of the world. Or to put it another way, today's evangelicals value worldliness.

Some of the things that evangelicals trust in but shouldn't include political power, judgmentalism, tribalism, popularity, and wealth. Many evangelicals have an unhealthy trust in worldly power. Such trust drives the pursuit of political power, but it also drives judgmentalism, which is a way to enforce conformity to tribal values. Tribalism is a form of power because it establishes norms of community expectation, as well as the community to enforce them. Popularity is another form of power because it yields influence and significance. And wealth is yet another type of power because it provides the ability to shape, create, buy, and influence the world.

My purpose here is not to paint all evangelicals with the same brush. But I am concerned that the problems I have identified are overrunning the evangelical movement today. So many of the major trends within evangelicalism support this diagnosis: evangelicals value worldliness and have placed their trust in worldly power.

TO KNOW HIM IS TO LOVE HIM

If this diagnosis is correct, what is the most effective way to course correct? The answer is straightforward: to look to Jesus yet again. He is the source of Christian faith; he is the center of evangelical theology; he is the foundation of everything that matters to the evangelical movement. I'm preaching to the choir right here, since the evangelical answer to every question is "Jesus!" But it still needs to be said. The worldliness of evangelical thinking and behavior must be critiqued by viewing Jesus afresh.

While the answer to every question might be Jesus, this does not mean that evangelicals view Jesus rightly. There is an "evangelical Jesus," who has been cast in evangelicalism's own image. So while the answer is Jesus, we cannot assume that we all share the same understanding of who he is. If the Jesus you're looking to seems like just another worldly leader, something has gone terribly wrong. The failures and fault lines of evangelicalism have prevented many from seeing Jesus clearly. Once we see him clearly, we will realize that there is no need for tribalism, no need for demonization, and no need for politicization. Jesus makes it possible to renounce worldliness and to embrace the power of love.

Beautiful, Shocking, Life Changing

They say attraction is stronger than persuasion. I realize that for many people Christianity seems anything but beautiful. Perhaps their experience of Christianity has been at the wrong end of judgmental Christians. Or Christians who try to impose their values on everyone. Or hypocritical Christians who are just as corrupt as anyone else. In my native Australia, society has virtually turned against Christianity as a morally bad thing to believe. Now secular society is judging Christians and calling us immoral, intolerant, and anti-intellectual. But the beauty of the Christian faith is grounded on the beauty of Jesus. I don't often call another man beautiful, but in Jesus' case it is both hard to deny and warranted. I am not referring to his appearance. (We don't have any descriptions of his appearance anyway.) I am referring to his character, his way with people, his teaching, his abilities, and his purpose. Even vehement critics of Christianity often acknowledge Jesus' striking beauty. They critique Christians for not living up to Jesus' teaching and example.

Jesus may be a controversial figure still, but one thing is not in doubt: he is still intriguing. Why are people still so interested in him? Remember that we are talking about a peasant from the Near East who had no formal education, no wealth, and no political power, did not publish anything, and did not travel farther than three hundred kilometers during his entire adult life. How could a man like that become the most famous person in history? How could a man like that have unparalleled influence in the history of humanity? How could a man like that become a dominant influence on culture, politics, morality, and religion— all before social media, TV, or newspapers? How was that even possible? Perhaps the easiest way to approach these questions is to realize that Jesus was shocking. Everything he did shocked people. Everything he said shocked people. Everywhere he went he shocked people.

Some of the things he did that shocked people include:

- hanging out with prostitutes
- kicking merchants out of the temple
- healing people with leprosy
- calling out religious hypocrites
- turning water into wine
- forgiving sins
- healing the blind
- raising the dead
- rising from the dead

Some of the things he said that shocked people include:

- that we should love our enemies
- that we should pray and give money in secret
- that God loves thieves and cheats
- that he is God's only Son
- that whoever believes in him will live forever
- that he would be betrayed and crucified

To top it all off, one of the last things he did was pray that God would forgive the people who crucified him—while they were crucifying him.

Jesus shocked people in the villages and in the city, he shocked the crowds and individuals, he shocked fishermen and the wealthy, he shocked Jews and Gentiles, he shocked his closest friends and family, and he shocked religious leaders and Roman soldiers. But Jesus did not shock them for the sake of it or because it was fun or just to get attention. He was no shock jock. He shocked people because what he did and said came with authority and power. He turned everything upside down.

His words were full of life-changing wisdom and insight. He did not follow the thought leaders or the religious leaders of his day. Instead, he shaped people's thought and taught them about God. He feared no one. His authority seemed to come from God himself, and he could back that up with the stunning things he could do. He was no ordinary man. He must have been the most extraordinary man anyone had ever known.

If you imagine someone who shocks everyone they meet, what sort of person comes to mind? Someone like Donald Trump or Miley Cyrus? My guess is you don't think of someone humble, gentle, compassionate, and kind—like the grandma next door. But Jesus was exactly like that. Yes, he was shocking. Yes, his teaching was radical. Yes, he stood up to aggressive people. But to ordinary people he was loving and approachable. To the ill he was kind and comforting. To the outcast he was welcoming and affirming. To the guilty he was merciful and forgiving. He didn't look down on anyone and he helped those who needed it. He was patient when people didn't understand him. He was never selfish or arrogant. He was not conceited or proud. Truly he was a remarkable mix of qualities—strong, confident, and challenging, while also gentle, humble, and kind.

Jesus was not like those charismatic leaders who are amazing in front of a crowd but aloof and unfriendly in person. I've known a few celebrities like that. People love them because they shine in front of a crowd. But in person they're a bit rude and stuck-up. It's a letdown, to be honest. But Jesus was both amazing in front of a crowd and amazing one to one. People felt his warmth and his concern. He could run rings around the religious elite, but he never used his intellect and knowledge to embarrass regular folk. For all his power and wisdom, he did not exalt himself or seek his own glory. Though he could have used his abilities for his own gain, he served others rather than himself.

Jesus is still shocking today even though we've had two thousand years to get used to him. Some things he said are less shocking now because they have become familiar. Other things are less shocking now because our culture has already been shaped by them and we take his ideas for granted. But there is still plenty about Jesus that is shocking today—like his resurrection from the dead.

Not only did Jesus shock people, he changed them. He did this through dramatic events such as enabling a crippled man to walk, but also through simple personal interactions like with a Samaritan woman who became a different person after one brief interchange with him. Many people were changed in an instant after encountering him. Others were changed gradually through hanging around him, like his closest disciples. Simon the fisherman is a classic example. Jesus gave him a new name—Peter—because he was set to become a different person through knowing Jesus. And he dramatically changed over a period of three years and became the foundational leader of the church in the years to follow.

It's easy to understand how Jesus changed people through healing and through other spectacular events. If you've been healed from leprosy or blindness or even been raised from the dead, then of course your life has been permanently changed for the better. Or if you saw Jesus walk on water, calm a storm, or feed five thousand people, I think you would be changed by those events too. But Jesus also changed people through his teaching. His teaching profoundly changed people because it altered the way they viewed life, the world, and God. Jesus' teaching turned accepted thought on its head, and he made people reassess their beliefs as well as what they held dear. Jesus' teaching has had a permanent effect on the world: he is constantly quoted (whether or not people realize they are quoting him), his stories are still widely known, and the ways he challenged the culture, religion, and customs of his day have influenced modern life immeasurably.

Truth Claims

No wonder people loved Jesus. Many adored him. But it's also no wonder that some rejected and hated him. Some things he said about himself were highly offensive to them because they did not believe him. To be sure, if he were not telling the truth, Jesus' claims would be grandiose and maybe a bit psychotic. But if he spoke the truth about himself, it was an entirely different situation. As C. S. Lewis famously wrote, Jesus was either a liar, a lunatic, or Lord. That's a helpful way to assess Jesus' claims about himself. If he was not God's only Son sent by God to reveal God to us, then either he was lying about it or he was delusional. Either way, he cannot be trusted. The only other option is that he spoke the truth and is therefore the Lord sent by his Father in heaven. The question is, What seems most likely? From what we know about Jesus, does he seem to be a liar? Does he seem crazy? Or does he sound like someone who speaks the truth, is in control of his faculties, and actually might be from beyond this world?

Jesus did amazing miracles. We're no doubt skeptical about these today, assuming that ancient people were easily fooled or that they believed in magic. Yet no one could deny Jesus' amazing feats—even his enemies acknowledged them. But he didn't do miracles to show off. He did them either to help people (healing the crippled, restoring lepers, giving sight to the blind, even raising the dead) or to reveal his divine nature (calming a storm, walking on water, feeding five thousand people). John called Jesus' miracles "signs" because they pointed to something: Jesus was sent by God and exercised God's power.

Jesus taught much about the kingdom of God. His listeners hoped for a renewed kingdom of Israel, where people would be free to worship their God without suffering foreign oppression. But Jesus taught about a kingdom that was not a political or economic entity. It was a spiritual kingdom in which people came under the authority of God's king. He explained that this kingdom is very different from the world's kingdoms. In this kingdom, the poor and humble are lifted up, while the rich and powerful are knocked down a peg or two. Treasure in the kingdom of God is measured by things like kindness and compassion. There are no enemies in the kingdom of God, only love and acceptance. And finally, the kingdom of God is hidden. It takes spiritual eyes to see it and it takes a heart for God to enter it.

Jesus taught that religious rules and outward appearances will not make someone right with God. Eating the right or wrong food is not the key, but what comes out of a person's heart shows who they really are. He taught that true devotion to God is seen in the way we treat other people, acting with compassion, righteousness, and truth. God despises hypocrites and loves to forgive those who regret their mistakes. God lifts up those who humble themselves and he humbles those who exalt themselves. Jesus taught that God's nature is always to have mercy.

Finally, Jesus taught that he would be betrayed, handed over to the Romans, and crucified, and then he would rise again in three days. He said that is how he would establish the kingdom of God—by dying for our sins and rising again that we might be put right with God. When Jesus was betrayed, mocked, flogged, and crucified, he did not retaliate or defend himself. He did not speak harshly to those who treated him like a criminal. Instead, he entrusted himself to God and peacefully went to his death for the sake of love. After three days in the tomb, Jesus rose again. This incredible miracle is not a make-believe story his disciples told so they could save face. It is as historically credible as any event in the ancient world, having been witnessed by hundreds of people, many of whom were not already followers of Jesus but became his followers as a result of what they saw. Their lives were turned around, like that of the apostle Paul—also known as Saul the Pharisee—whose mission had been to hunt down and arrest Jesus' followers. He hated Christians and oversaw their deaths. But after encountering the risen Jesus, he became a follower of Jesus himself. And not just any follower but one of the greatest apostles, theologians, and missionaries the world has ever seen. Paul wrote thirteen books of the New Testament. If you doubt the resurrection of Jesus, you will need to account for the radical transformation of Paul, who went from being Christianity's number-one enemy to its greatest teacher (after Jesus himself).

Influence and Significance

Influence is measured by how much someone affects other people. Jesus had a profound effect on thousands of people, so on that measure he was very influential. Significance is measured by how much a person's life changes things. Jesus' life, death, and resurrection permanently shaped history. On that measure, he was incredibly significant. To be sure, influence and significance are not necessarily good things. After all, Adolf Hitler was very influential and significant, but most people wish he had never been born. But when the right people have influence and significance, they can do immeasurable good. Think of the likes of Michelangelo, Galileo, Isaac Newton, J. S. Bach, Abraham Lincoln, Mother Teresa, Martin Luther King Jr., Desmond Tutu. People who changed the world for the better. And Jesus sits at the top of any list of people who've had a positive influence on humanity. No one else in history can claim to have had as much influence for good as Jesus.

There is abundant evidence of the goodness of Jesus' influence. When people were changed by encountering him, they were changed for the better. Like the tax collector who decided to pay back fourfold everyone he had stolen money from, and gave away half his possessions to the poor. Like Peter, who wanted to violently overthrow the Romans and later learned to love his enemies. Like Paul, who was also violent (against Christians) but later practiced nonviolence even when he was attacked. And like countless others throughout history who have learned from Jesus how to love, how to put others ahead of themselves, how to forgive, how to reconcile, how to show compassion, and how to make peace. Many of the great ones of later history were inspired by Jesus. So Dallas Willard and Gary Black Jr. comment, Jesus "is and has remained the hero of so many of our celebrated heroes across time."[1] We could even say that their influence and significance are simply the results of Jesus' influence and significance.

There are many reasons why Jesus matters today. First is the purely historical reason. If Jesus was one of the most influential people in human history, any thoughtful person will want to know something about who he was, why he was so influential, and what influence he had. We should understand how our culture has been shaped by his influence, including our own worldviews and thought worlds. Even if someone had never heard of Jesus, he has indirectly contributed to their understanding of life in the world, so it would be wise to learn more about him. Second is the religious reason. Whether or not someone considers themselves a religious person, religion is a big part of this world. Since Jesus is the founder of the biggest religion in history, it is worth the time to become more acquainted with him. Third is the personal reason. Jesus has been changing lives for two thousand years. He's still changing lives. He can offer profound insight into our humanity, into our struggle against injustice, and into our quest for love. Jesus challenges our assumptions about life, about other people, and about God. He offers a vision of what's important in life. He brings freedom from rules and religious oppression. He can introduce us to ourselves. He can introduce us to God.

Evangelicals must look afresh to Jesus. The evangelical movement must be refashioned in Jesus' image, rather than cast Jesus in its image. The portrait of Jesus we've been examining offers self-evident critique of a movement that has lost sight of its first love.

FIRST LOVE

How would reenvisioning evangelicals' first love reshape their character, mission, and public image? How would it look for the evangelical movement as a whole to be refashioned in Jesus' image? How would a renunciation of worldliness and worldly power heal the fault lines that threaten to destroy evangelicalism? Take another look at the fault lines we listed earlier in this chapter, but this time followed by one-liners from Jesus. One-liners don't convey the whole story and can be taken out of context, but they do offer a sharp summary of the case Jesus brings against evangelicals.

- Fault line: American evangelicalism has become politicized to the extent that its spiritual nature has been distorted, fueled by the assumption that political power will transform American culture.
  » Jesus: "My kingdom is not of this world" (John 18:36).
- Fault line: Evangelicals tend to uphold an "us versus them" mentality toward outsiders, shaped by a lack of self-sacrificial love and acceptance of others.
  » Jesus: "Love your enemies and pray for those who persecute you" (Matthew 5:44).
- Fault line: Evangelicalism suffers from the perception and reality of judgmentalism, forged by self-righteousness and a lack of humility.
  » Jesus: "Do not judge, or you too will be judged" (Matthew 7:1).
- Fault line: Evangelicals are often highly divisive, exacerbating theological and cultural divisions that create tribal boundaries established by tribal ways of reading the Bible.
  » Jesus: "By this everyone will know that you are my disciples, if you love one another" (John 13:35).
- Fault line: Evangelicals have an understood code of acceptable and unacceptable sins, created through tribal values rather than the priorities of the Bible.

> » Jesus: "You have neglected the more important matters of the law—justice, mercy and faithfulness. . . . You strain out a gnat but swallow a camel" (Matthew 23:23–24).

- Fault line: Evangelicals tend to shoot their wounded by the way they treat marriage failure, divorce, and remarriage.

> » Jesus: "Let any one of you who is without sin be the first to throw a stone at her" (John 8:7).

- Fault line: Evangelicals celebrate an unhealthy church model—the megachurch—that has adopted our cultural fascination with celebrity, size, consumerism, and entertainment.

> » Jesus: "Whoever wants to become great among you must be your servant" (Mark 10:43).

- Fault line: The popular face of evangelicalism has been overrun by fringe personalities peddling false gospels aimed at manipulating their followers to forge their own fortunes.

> » Jesus: "Many will say to me on that day, 'Lord, Lord, did we not prophesy in your name and in your name drive out demons and in your name perform many miracles?' Then I will tell them plainly, 'I never knew you. Away from me, you evildoers!'" (Matthew 7:22–23).

As I suggested earlier, these evangelical fault lines arise from valuing worldliness and trusting in worldly power. Such worldliness derives from losing sight of Jesus. He models otherworldly values and otherworldly power. He teaches his followers to do the same if they are to do good in this world. If they take their cue from Jesus, evangelicals will resist worldliness and embrace the values of the kingdom of God: humility, compassion, justice, mercy, and love. Evangelicals should spurn worldly power and trust in the power that comes from the love of God in Christ. This power is cruciform, self-sacrificial, service-oriented love that transforms people from the inside out.

Imagine an evangelicalism known for such things.

Biblical scholar Mark Glanville and his brother Luke Glanville, a professor of international relations, recount an event in which evangelicals lived up to our imagination.

In 2017, armed bikers were planning to rally outside a mosque in Phoenix, to burn Qur'ans, to burn images of Muhammad, and to shout insults. Hundreds of participants had signed up on Facebook. . . . The organizers encouraged people to come prepared to use their firearms.

Two faith leaders, friends of ours, Jim Mullins and Adam Estle, spotted the event on Facebook. They consulted with the president of the mosque, with whom they already had a friendship. Then, just twenty-four hours before the rally was due to start, they called upon Christians to gather at the mosque to be a prayerful and peaceful presence. Their aim was to create a physical barrier of protection with their bodies and a spiritual wall of protection with their prayers. As Jim put it: "Before a bullet could pierce the body of a Muslim person, it would first have to pass through the body of a Christian."

Jim and Adam were deeply moved when around two hundred Christians arrived outside the mosque, wearing blue T-shirts to identify themselves. Christ followers numbered about the same as the protesters. They formed a line between the protestors and the mosque. They prayed deeply, and they engaged the angriest and loudest protesters in conversation, listening carefully to their concerns.[2]

Followers of Jesus are called to pick up their crosses and follow him (Mark 8:34). Given that we know what Jesus did with his cross, this is obviously a call to be willing to go to our own deaths. Just as Jesus laid down his life for others, so will his followers. Such self-sacrifice not only is offered for those who are like us or are liked by us but also extends to all regardless of religion, political persuasion, wealth, sex, or ethnicity. The pattern of the cross demonstrates God's love for the Muslims at the mosque, the angry bikers with guns, anyone watching on TV, and everyone else the world round. If evangelicals are willing to shake themselves free of the instincts driving their entanglement with partisan politics, self-preservation, worldly power, and phobias of people who are different, there may be hope yet. But they must *follow Jesus*.

WHAT'S IN A NAME?

In 1984, Thomas Howard wrote in his book *Evangelical Is Not Enough*, "The word *evangelical* is an ancient and noble one, but it has become somewhat rickety. It has too many meanings. In our own time it sprang into popular use with the presidency of Jimmy Carter, when anyone who claimed to be born again seemed to fall into the category. The press often used the word as a synonym for middle-class religion."[3]

The situation for the term *evangelical* has not improved in nearly forty years. It has gotten worse. In 2016, Russell Moore wrote in the *Washington Post*, "The word 'evangelical' has become almost meaningless this year, and in many ways the word itself is at the moment subverting the gospel of Jesus Christ. . . . We have been too willing to look the other way when the word 'evangelical' has been co-opted by heretics and lunatics."[4]

Historian Thomas Kidd says that "'evangelical' now basically means *whites who consider themselves religious and who vote Republican*,"[5] while influential pastor Timothy Keller says "the word is nearly synonymous with 'hypocrite.'"[6] What should evangelicals call themselves if *evangelical* is no longer a term with which they can happily identify?

Some people really care about labels. I understand the appeal; labels help us to organize people, ideas, and things into categories we can understand. From a theological perspective, we could say that labels find their origin in God's commission of the first humans to name every living creature (Genesis 2:19). Naming is an important part of understanding. The growth of human knowledge largely consists of giving names to species, physical phenomena, linguistic phenomena, psychological phenomena, and so on. Names provide a shortcut for talking about things that would require a lengthier description if the name did not exist. Like saying, "You know, that hairy four-legged creature that sniffs and barks?" "Oh, you mean the *dog*!" It's much easier to use the label *dog* than to describe the dog every time you want to talk about a dog. (Just think about how difficult that sentence would be if we had no word for dog.) I'm not saying that evangelicals are dogs. But there is a parallel. It's easier to use a label that supposedly matches someone's beliefs than to describe their beliefs every time you want to refer to what they believe. It's easier to say "evangelical" than to say "a Christian who believes in the Bible as the authoritative Word of God and is described by Bebbington's quadrilateral of conversionism, activism, biblicism, and crucicentrism." So there's a place for labels. Communication and understanding would be much more difficult without them.

But what happens when a label fails? A truism of linguistic evolution is that words change their meaning according to usage. I find it frustrating when someone (typically a teenager) says, "I literally died." If you literally died, you would not be able to misuse the word *literally* because you'd be dead. But because so many people now use *literally* to mean figuratively, the meaning has changed. Even the *Oxford English Dictionary* now recognizes this change of meaning. Under the possible meanings of the word is—you guessed it—the figurative meaning![7] Meaning is determined by usage and there's nothing we can do about that. I can no more control what the word *evangelical* means than I can decide what *literally* means. Both words mean what the wider population use them to mean. As such, evangelicals have a problem with the label *evangelical*, whether they realize it or not. They identify themselves as evangelicals because they think they know what *evangelical* means. But it doesn't mean what they think it means. Maybe it did once, but no longer. If the public thinks that Paula White is an evangelical, then real evangelicals are not evangelicals anymore.

The same thing happened to the label *fundamentalism*. Originally, *fundamentalism* referred to a kind of Christianity that focused on the fundamentals of faith—core convictions that a majority of Christians would happily accept.[8] But the fundamentalist movement became increasingly preoccupied with issues that were not fundamental to Christian faith, such as whether Genesis can be interpreted literally in the face of modern science.[9] In the infamous Scopes Trial of 1925 (*The State of Tennessee v. John Thomas Scopes*), fundamentalists claimed that the Bible overrules scientific claims such as evolution. After the Scopes Trial, *fundamentalism* no longer meant what it once did. Because of the publicity of the trial, the word would thereafter be known as a type of Christianity that insists on a literal reading of the Bible, which overrules all other means of knowledge.[10] And that's why so many fundamentalists rebranded themselves as evangelicals in the 1940s. Du Mez notes that with the emergence of the National Association of Evangelicals, founded by fundamentalists in 1942, "'evangelical' came to connote a more forward-looking alternative to the militant, separatist fundamentalism that had become an object of ridicule."[11] Fundamentalism ain't what it used to be.

If fundamentalists were smart enough to become evangelicals, are evangelicals smart enough to become whatever the next label will be? That's the question now to consider. As far as I can see, there are three options: keep the label, redefine the label, and ditch the label.

Keep the Label

Some people care about labels, especially when they've put a lot of self-identification into them. Many evangelicals are passionate about identifying themselves as evangelicals. The label has a long and rich history, and it was coined to put the gospel of Jesus (the *evangel* in biblical Greek) at the center of Christian faith. Some people have lost friends because of the label or fought difficult battles for it. Perhaps they've named a book with it or taught at an institution named with it. Some have written books about who is an evangelical and how the label should properly be understood. There are all kinds of reasons why people do not want to give up the label.

I'm sympathetic to evangelicals' attachment to being known as evangelicals. I feel the pain of letting go a label that once meant so much. I feel the discomfort of not knowing what to call myself anymore. I feel the same pull of wanting to correct others about what the term means. But it is a futile exercise. Some of these folks might have been quite happy to call themselves fundamentalists in 1922, but they would be repulsed at the thought in 2022. That's how it will be for evangelicals in time. The label is slipping away, and the sooner we accept it, the better. But to those who will resist my impenetrable logic, I say good luck.

Redefine the Label

The ambitious evangelical might decide to redefine the label so that it means what they want it to mean. This way they can keep the label and avoid the negative connotations that plague it. The problem is that no one can control language. We might define how we want to use a term, and tell others that's how we're using it, but that will do absolutely nothing to change the meaning of the word, which is what the public understands it to mean.

The only way to change the meaning of a label is to massively influence the public somehow so that they begin to understand the term differently. But even if that were possible, there is no clear way to achieve the desired outcome, since language evolution happens at a subconscious, communal level. Telling people directly what a word means rarely works. A widely respected and wildly popular figure such as Billy Graham did much for the term *evangelical* because he was beyond reproach, he was consulted by every president from Eisenhower to Clinton, and he preached to hundreds of millions of people around the world. If anyone wanted to know what an evangelical was, they could look to Billy Graham. But as much as evangelicals might wish they had another Billy Graham to represent them, they don't and likely won't. He was not a once-in-a-generation figure, he was once in a century. But even with Billy Graham there was confusion about the term *evangelical*; most thought it means "evangelistic," partly because Graham was an evangelist. But now with so much noise about evangelicals during the Trump era, it seems impossible to counteract the misunderstandings. I guess evangelicals could pray for a miracle to recover their beloved label, but I think God has better things to do.

Ditch the Label

Thomas Kidd says, "In public references to ourselves, it is probably time to put 'evangelical' on the shelf."[12] If you ditch the label, where does that leave you? I'm fortunate that I can simply call myself an Anglican. But many evangelicals do not belong to a denomination. Part of the popularity of the evangelical label was that it transcended denominational affiliations or substituted for them. Many evangelical churches are independent and nondenominational, and their evangelical status has helped to identify their convictions. So, again, if you ditch the label, where does that leave you?

Some adopt the term *post-evangelical*, but that doesn't say much except what you used to be. It seems that most who use that label tend to mean that their theological convictions have changed. The popular Twitter handle #exvangelical seems to be used by people who are repulsed by the culture of evangelicalism, whether or not their theological convictions have shifted.[13] (By the way, I think *exangelical* is better.)[14] These labels seem to appeal to people who not only want to distance themselves from evangelicalism but want to be *seen* to distance themselves. Their former evangelical status is explicitly renounced. For others, it's not important to repudiate their former label. They just want a label that works now. I've seen some attempts to find an alternative to *evangelical*, but I don't know how successful they will be. Some examples include *Bible-believing Christian, conservative Christian, reformed Protestant,* and *gospel Christian.* I'm not sure if those work as well as *evangelical* used to. In the end, however, words mean what we use them to mean. Whatever term catches on will be filled with the meaning that people give it. It might as well be *pink elephant Jesus freaks*—it doesn't really matter.

In the meantime, a well-meaning Christian who no longer wants to identify as an evangelical might feel a bit lost at sea—like the musician Prince after he repudiated his name and had to be referred to as "the artist formerly known as Prince." It's a bit clunky. But maybe this is all a good thing. It could be an opportunity to eschew the stock we put in labels. It could be an opportunity to diffuse the power of tribal membership over us. It could be an opportunity to strip things down to the fundamentals of faith—following Jesus, studying the Bible, and loving others. But this could also be a spiritually tricky time, especially if believers stop engaging in fellowship with other believers. Over time, that could lead to abandoning the faith altogether, as many post-evangelicals and exangelicals ultimately end up doing. For me, finding an Anglican church that seeks to follow Jesus, study the Scriptures, and love others is just what I needed. I appreciate the liturgy and its nontribal feel. I benefit from attending a church that is not trying to coerce action in conformity to tribal expectations but allows Jesus to do his work in our hearts and minds. And people without a label fit in just fine.

NOTES

Introduction

1. Peter Wehner, "Evangelicals Made a Bad Bargain with Trump," *The Atlantic*, October 18, 2020, www.theatlantic.com/ideas /archive/2020/10/the-evangelical-movements-bad-bargain /616760/.
2. Wehner, "Evangelicals Made a Bad Bargain."
3. Terry Shoemaker, "White Gen X and Millennial Evangelicals Are Losing Faith in the Conservative Culture Wars," *Conversation*, June 22, 2021, https://theconversation.com/white -gen-x-and-millennial-evangelicals-are-losing-faith-in-the -conservative-culture-wars-162407.
4. David P. Gushee, "The Problem with White Evangelicalism Is Not Jesus," *Faith and Leadership*, October 27, 2020, https://faithandleadership.com/david-p-gushee-problem-white -evangelicalism-not-jesus.
5. This is the title of a helpful introduction to the question by historian Thomas Kidd. Thomas S. Kidd, *Who Is an Evangelical? The History of a Movement in Crisis* (New Haven, CT: Yale Univ. Press, 2019).
6. David W. Bebbington, *Evangelicalism in Modern Britain: A History from the 1730s to the 1980s* (London: Routledge, 1989), 2–3.
7. George M. Marsden, *Understanding Fundamentalism and Evangelicalism* (Grand Rapids: Eerdmans, 1991), 1–2.

8. Marsden, *Understanding Fundamentalism and Evangelicalism*, 4.

9. Alan Wolfe, *The Transformation of Religion in America: How We Actually Live Our Faith* (New York: Free Press, 2003), 36.

10. Wolfe, *Transformation of Religion in America*, 143.

11. Kristin Kobes Du Mez, *Jesus and John Wayne: How White Evangelicals Corrupted a Faith and Fractured a Nation* (New York: Liveright, 2020), 297–98.

12. Mark A. Noll, "Introduction: One Word but Three Crises," in *Evangelicals: Who They Have Been, Are Now, and Could Be*, ed. Mark A. Noll, David W. Bebbington, and George M. Marsden (Grand Rapids: Eerdmans, 2019), Kindle loc. 266.

13. Noll, "Introduction: One Word but Three Crises," Kindle loc. 266.

14. George M. Marsden, "The Evangelical Denomination," in *Evangelicals: Who They Have Been, Are Now, and Could Be* , ed. Mark A. Noll, David W. Bebbington, and George M. Marsden (Grand Rapids: Eerdmans, 2019), Kindle loc. 594.

15. Ross Douthat, *Bad Religion: How We Became a Nation of Heretics* (New York: Free Press, 2012), 3.

Chapter 1: God and Country

1. E. J. Dionne Jr. and William A. Galston, "The Old and New Politics of Faith: Religion and the 2010 Election," Brookings Institution, November 17, 2010, www.brookings.edu/research/the -old-and-new-politics-of-faith-religion-and-the-2010-election.

2. Mark A. Noll, *A History of Christianity in the United States and Canada* (Grand Rapids: Eerdmans, 1992), 31–53.

3. Francis J. Bremer, *John Winthrop: America's Forgotten Founding Father* (Oxford: Oxford Univ. Press, 2005), 171.

4. George Marsden, *Understanding Fundamentalism and Evangelicalism* (Grand Rapids: Eerdmans, 1991), 85.

5. Mark A. Signorelli, "A City upon a Hill," *Front Porch Republic*, March 28, 2011, www.frontporchrepublic.com/2011/03/a-city -upon-a-hill/, italics in original.

6. Jim Wallis, *God's Politics: Why the American Right Gets It Wrong and the Left Doesn't Get It* (Oxford: Lion, 2005), xx.

7. Wallis, *God's Politics*, xx.

8. Kristin Kobes Du Mez, *Jesus and John Wayne: How White Evangelicals Corrupted a Faith and Fractured a Nation* (New York: Liveright, 2020), 11.

9. Du Mez, *Jesus and John Wayne*, 36.

10. Thomas S. Kidd, *Who Is an Evangelical? The History of a Movement in Crisis* (New Haven, CT: Yale Univ. Press, 2019), 154.

11. James Davison Hunter, *To Change the World: The Irony, Tragedy, and Possibility of Christianity in the Late Modern World* (Oxford: Oxford Univ. Press, 2010), 42.

12. Wallis, *God's Politics*, 3.

13. John Fea, *Believe Me: The Evangelical Road to Donald Trump* (Grand Rapids: Eerdmans, 2018), 16.

14. "Trump expanded his support among White evangelical Protestants slightly, winning 84% of their vote in 2020 after receiving 77% in 2016, when he ran against Hillary Clinton." Justin Nortey, "Most White Americans Who Regularly Attend Worship Services Voted for Trump in 2020," Pew Research Center, August 30, 2021, www.pewresearch.org/fact-tank/2021/08/30/most-white-americans-who-regularly-attend-worship-services-voted-for-trump-in-2020/.

15. Du Mez, *Jesus and John Wayne*, 3.

16. Fea, *Believe Me*, 60.

17. Phyllis Schlafly, "Will We Allow Clinton to Redefine the Presidency?" *Eagle Forum*, February 11, 1998, https://eagleforum.org/column/1998/feb98/98-02-11.html, cited in Du Mez, *Jesus and John Wayne*, 143.

18. James Dobson, "An Evangelical Response to Bill Clinton" (1998), in *The Columbia Documentary History of Religion in America Since 1945*, ed. Paul Harvey and Phillip Goff (New York: Columbia Univ. Press, 2007), 303–7, cited in Du Mez, *Jesus and John Wayne*, 143.

19. "Presidential Historians Survey 2021: Moral Authority," *C-Span*, www.c-span.org/presidentsurvey2021/?category=4.

20. Jonathan Merritt, "Trump-Loving Christians Owe Bill Clinton an Apology," *Atlantic*, August 10, 2016, www.theatlantic.com /politics/archive/2016/08/evangelical-christians-trump-bill -clinton-apology/495224/.

21. Merritt, "Trump-Loving Christians."

22. Katherine Stewart, "Why Trump Reigns as King Cyrus," *New York Times*, December 31, 2018, www.nytimes.com/2018/12/31 /opinion/trump-evangelicals-cyrus-king.html.

23. Du Mez, *Jesus and John Wayne*, 3–4.

24. Du Mez, *Jesus and John Wayne*, 4. Du Mez points to the following research to establish these points: Jim Lobe, "Politics—U.S.: Conservative Christians Biggest Backers of Iraq War," Inter Press Service, October 9, 2002; "The Religious Dimensions of the Torture Debate," Pew Research Center, May 7, 2009; Kate Shellnutt, "Packing in the Pews: The Connection between God and Guns," *Christianity Today*, November 8, 2017; Betsy Cooper et al., "How Americans View Immigrants, and What They Want from Immigration Reform: Findings from the American Values Atlas," Public Religion Research Institute, March 29, 2016; "Data Shows How Passionate and Partisan Americans Are about the Border Wall," Public Religion Research Institute, January 8, 2019.

25. Wallis, *God's Politics*, 3.

26. Robert P. Jones, "The Evangelicals and the Great Trump Hope," *New York Times*, July 11, 2016, cited in Du Mez, *Jesus and John Wayne*, 13–14.

27. Kidd, *Who Is an Evangelical?* 71.

28. Kidd, *Who Is an Evangelical?* 72.

29. Ross Douthat, *Bad Religion: How We Became a Nation of Heretics* (New York: Free Press, 2012), 37, italics in original.

30. Douthat, *Bad Religion*, 139.

31. Kidd, *Who Is an Evangelical?* 73.

32. Kidd, *Who Is an Evangelical?* 147.

33. Douthat, *Bad Religion*, 122–23.
34. Sarah Kliff, "The American Abortion Rate Is at an All-Time Low," *Vox*, December 3, 2018, www.vox.com/2018/12/3/18119528/abortion-rate-decline-2018-birth-control-iud-pill.
35. Gabrielle Levy, "Abortion Rates: Where and Why They're Falling," *U.S. News and World Report*, March 21, 2018, www.usnews.com/news/data-mine/articles/2018-03-21/abortion-rates-where-and-why-theyre-falling.
36. Susheela Singh et al, "Abortion Worldwide 2017: Uneven Progress and Unequal Access," *Guttmacher Institute*, March 2018, www.guttmacher.org/report/abortion-worldwide-2017.
37. Kara Fox, "How US Gun Culture Compares with the World," *CNN*, August 6, 2019, https://edition.cnn.com/2017/10/03/americas/us-gun-statistics/.
38. Wallis, *God's Politics*, 32.
39. Edward W. Klink, *John*, Zondervan Exegetical Commentary on the New Testament (Grand Rapids: Zondervan, 2016), 764.
40. D. A. Carson, *The Gospel according to John*, Pillar New Testament Commentary (Grand Rapids: Eerdmans, 1991), 594.
41. Scot McKnight, *The Letter to the Colossians*, New International Commentary on the New Testament (Grand Rapids: Eerdmans, 2018), 126.
42. Constantine R. Campbell, *Paul and the Hope of Glory: An Exegetical and Theological Study* (Grand Rapids: Zondervan Academic, 2020), 91–92.
43. Thomas R. Schreiner, *1 and 2 Peter and Jude*, Christian Standard Commentary (Nashville: Holman Reference, 2020), 128.
44. Oliver O'Donovan, *The Desire of the Nations: Rediscovering the Roots of Political Theology* (Cambridge: Cambridge Univ. Press, 1996), 251.
45. O'Donovan, *Desire of the Nations*, 250.
46. Wallis, *God's Politics*, 32.
47. Wallis, *God's Politics*, 32.
48. Jonathan T. Pennington, *The Sermon on the Mount and Human*

Flourishing: A Theological Commentary (Grand Rapids: Baker Academic, 2017), 167–68.

49. Wallis, *God's Politics*, 61–64.

50. Wallis, *God's Politics*, 64, italics in original.

51. Wallis, *God's Politics*, 64.

52. Wallis, *God's Politics*, 64.

53. Mark Dever, *Discipling: How to Help Others Follow Jesus* (Wheaton, IL: Crossway, 2016), 13.

54. Randall Balmer, *God in the White House: A History; How Faith Shaped the Presidency from John F. Kennedy to George W. Bush* (New York: HarperOne, 2008), 167, italics in original.

55. David P. Gushee, *After Evangelicalism: The Path to a New Christianity* (Louisville: Westminster John Knox, 2020), 144–49.

56. Rome was more barbaric than today's Western cultures, however, and this change is largely because the West has been shaped profoundly by Christianity. We no longer have legalized slavery, bloody gladiatorial games, or the ruthless *pax Romana*. And unwanted babies are not regularly tossed onto garbage dumps. (Today's abortions are more sanitized.) See Larry W. Hurtado, *Destroyer of the Gods: Early Christian Distinctiveness in the Roman World* (Waco: Baylor Univ. Press, 2016), 144–50.

57. Rodney Stark, *The Rise of Christianity: How the Obscure, Marginal Jesus Movement Became the Dominant Religious Force in the Western World in a Few Centuries* (New York: HarperOne, 1997), 2.

58. Helen Rhee, *Loving the Poor, Saving the Rich: Wealth, Poverty, and Early Christian Formation* (Grand Rapids: Baker Academic, 2012), 179.

59. Stark, *Rise of Christianity*, 188–89, 209–15.

60. Edwin A. Judge, "The Quest for Mercy in Late Antiquity," in *God Who Is Rich in Mercy: Essays Presented to D. B. Knox*, ed. P. T. O'Brien and D. G. Peterson (Sydney: Macquarie Univ. Press, 1986), 107.

61. Rhee, *Loving the Poor*, 107–17.

62. Rhee, *Loving the Poor*, 128–31.
63. Hurtado, *Destroyer of the Gods*, 103.
64. Emperor Julian, "Fragment of a Letter to a Priest," in *The Works of the Emperor Julian*, Loeb Classical Library 29, 2:338.

Chapter 2: Exclusion Zones

1. Mazoe Ford, "Sydney Anglican Archbishop Defends $1M Donation to Same-Sex Marriage No Campaign," *ABC News*, October 11, 2017, www.abc.net.au/news/2017-10-11/archbishop -defends-1m-donation-to-same-sex-marriage-no-campaign /9040322.
2. See, for example, Todd A. Wilson, *Mere Sexuality: Rediscovering the Christian Vision of Sexuality* (Grand Rapids: Zondervan, 2017); Timothy C. Tennent, *For the Body: Recovering a Theology of Gender, Sexuality, and the Human Body* (Grand Rapids: Zondervan, 2020).
3. See Preston Sprinkle, gen. ed., *Two Views on Homosexuality, the Bible, and the Church*, Counterpoints: Bible and Theology (Grand Rapids: Zondervan, 2016).
4. Hunter Schwarz, "Married Same-Sex Couples Makes Up Less Than One Half of One Percent of All Married Couples in the U.S.," *Washington Post*, September 22, 2014, www.washington post.com/blogs/govbeat/wp/2014/09/22/married-same-sex -couples-make-up-less-than-one-half-of-one-percent-of-all -married-couples-in-the-u-s/.
5. Christine E. Gudorf, "The Bible and Science on Sexuality," in *Homosexuality, Science, and the "Plain Sense" of Scripture*, ed. David L. Balch (Grand Rapids: Eerdmans, 2000), 134.
6. Kelli Bender, "California Man Planning to Wed His Beloved Cat to Raise Money for Los Angeles Animal Shelter," People, May 19, 2020, https://people.com/pets/california-man-cat -wedding-raise-money-animal-shelter/.
7. Arin Greenwood, "Meet the Woman Who's Been Happily Married to Two Cats for More Than a Decade," *HuffPost*,

January 12, 2015, www.huffpost.com/entry/woman-married-to
-cats-barbarella-buchner_n_6455472.

8. David P. Gushee, *After Evangelicalism: The Path to a New Christianity* (Louisville: Westminster John Knox, 2020), 127.

9. See Mark G. Toulouse, "Muddling Through: The Church and Sexuality/Homosexuality," in *Homosexuality, Science, and the "Plain Sense" of Scripture*, ed. David L. Balch (Grand Rapids: Eerdmans, 2000), 6–42.

10. Gushee, *After Evangelicalism*, 135.

11. Gushee summarizes evangelical evasions of the reality of same-sex attraction: "Same-sex attraction was a delusion. It was temporary. It was demon possession. It was willful. It was changeable. The delusion could be cured, the temporary feeling could be made to pass, the demons could be exorcised, the will could be changed. Gay people could be 'repaired.'" Gushee, *After Evangelicalism*, 129.

12. See Stanton L. Jones and Mark A. Yarhouse, "The Use, Misuse, and Abuse of Science in the Ecclesiastical Homosexuality Debates," in *Homosexuality, Science, and the "Plain Sense" of Scripture*, ed. David L. Balch (Grand Rapids: Eerdmans, 2000), 73–120. Notable: "It seems most reasonable to conclude that genetic, brain structure, prenatal hormonal, and psychological/familial factors may each be a facilitating or contributing cause of homosexual orientation in some individuals. . . . Some of these influencing factors may be genetic in origin, but genetic influence may not mean a 'sexual orientation gene'; rather, other high-order traits may dispose some children to atypical social relationships, patterns of psychological identification, and so forth" (104–5).

13. Hebrew anthropology is foundational to Christian approaches to personhood, and both are holistic, resisting the popular ancient Greek notion that the body and soul can, and ideally should, be separated. Whatever else a holistic anthropology means, it must at least mean that we cannot determine our personhood from

biology alone. There is a complex interplay between mind, body, and spirit, and no one is even close to unlocking its mysteries. An obvious example is the New Testament insistence on the fallenness of human "flesh." But the flesh is not about the body *per se*. The flesh has implications for the body, but it is not the same as the body. It permeates the whole person, including body, mind, and spirit. And Christian salvation does not overturn such fallenness—at least, not until the promised resurrection when the body will be resurrected, but the flesh will not. This means that human fallenness is not purely a biological issue; it is a human issue. Likewise, homosexuality and transgenderism are not purely biological issues; they are human issues.

14. Dennis R. Edwards, *Might from the Margins: The Gospel's Power to Turn the Tables on Injustice* (Harrisonburg, VA: Herald Press, 2020), 25.

15. Jemar Tisby, *The Color of Compromise: The Truth about the American Church's Complicity in Racism* (Grand Rapids: Zondervan Reflective, 2019), 77–78.

16. Gushee, *After Evangelicalism*, 158.

17. Robert P. Jones, *White Too Long: The Legacy of White Supremacy in American Christianity* (New York: Simon and Schuster, 2020), 2.

18. Tisby, *Color of Compromise*, 100.

19. Tisby, *Color of Compromise*, 149.

20. Jones, *White Too Long*, 43–45.

21. Gushee, *After Evangelicalism*, 158–61.

22. Jemar Tisby, *How to Fight Racism: Courageous Christianity and the Journey toward Racial Justice* (Grand Rapids: Zondervan Reflective, 2021), 26.

23. Jones, *White Too Long*, 10.

24. Tisby, *Color of Compromise*, 16.

25. George Schroeder, "Seminary Presidents Reaffirm BFM, Declare CRT Incompatible," *Baptist Press*, November 30, 2020, www.baptistpress.com/resource-library/news/seminary -presidents-reaffirm-bfm-declare-crt-incompatible/.

26. Timothy Keller, *Generous Justice: How God's Grace Makes Us Just* (London: Hodder and Stoughton, 2010), 127.

27. Voddie T. Baucham Jr., *Fault Lines: The Social Justice Movement and Evangelicalism's Looming Catastrophe* (Washington: Salem, 2021), 4–5, 66–83, 206–16.

28. Jonathan T. Pennington, *The Sermon on the Mount and Human Flourishing: A Theological Commentary* (Grand Rapids: Baker Academic, 2017), 201.

29. Scot McKnight, *A Fellowship of Differents: Showing the World God's Design for Life Together* (Grand Rapids: Zondervan, 2014), 53–59.

30. Amy-Jill Levine and Ben Witherington III, *The Gospel of Luke*, New Cambridge Bible Commentary (Cambridge: Cambridge Univ. Press, 2018), 291.

31. Levine and Witherington, *Gospel of Luke*, 285–87.

32. Levine and Witherington, *Gospel of Luke*, 293.

33. Keller, *Generous Justice*, 67.

34. Pennington, *Sermon on the Mount*, 200.

35. Scot McKnight, *Kingdom Conspiracy: Returning to the Radical Mission of the Local Church* (Grand Rapids: Brazos, 2014), 111.

36. Tisby, *How to Fight Racism*, 101–2.

37. Dallas Willard and Gary Black Jr., *The Divine Conspiracy Continued: Fulfilling God's Kingdom on Earth* (New York: HarperOne, 2014), 117.

Chapter 3: Bad Judgment

1. Rosaria Champagne Butterfield, "My Train Wreck Conversion," *Christianity Today*, February 7, 2013, www.christianitytoday.com /ct/2013/january-february/my-train-wreck-conversion.html.

2. Barna Group, "A New Generation Expresses Its Skepticism and Frustration with Christianity," Barna, September 21, 2007, www.barna.com/research/a-new-generation-expresses-its -skepticism-and-frustration-with-christianity/.

3. Jonathan Merritt, "Some of the Most Visible Christians in

America Are Failing the Coronavirus Test," *Atlantic*, April 24, 2020, www.theatlantic.com/ideas/archive/2020/04/christian -cruelty-face-covid-19/610477/.

4. Grant R. Osborne, *Matthew*, Zondervan Exegetical Commentary on the New Testament (Grand Rapids: Zondervan, 2010), 257–58.

5. Jonathan T. Pennington, *The Sermon on the Mount and Human Flourishing: A Theological Commentary* (Grand Rapids: Baker Academic, 2017), 255.

6. Rodney Reeves, *Matthew*, The Story of God Bible Commentary (Grand Rapids: Zondervan, 2017), 143–44.

7. Darrell L. Bock, *Luke*, vol. 1, 1:1–9:50, Baker Exegetical Commentary on the New Testament (Grand Rapids: Baker, 1994), 695.

8. Bock, *Luke*, 698–99.

9. Osborne, *Matthew*, 257–58, 685–87.

10. Roy E. Ciampa and Brian S. Rosner, *The First Letter to the Corinthians*, Pillar New Testament Commentary (Grand Rapids: Eerdmans, 2010), 219–22.

11. Frederick William Danker, Walter Bauer, William F. Arndt, and F. Wilbur Gingrich, *A Greek-English Lexicon of the New Testament and Other Early Christian Literature*, 3rd ed. (Chicago: Univ. of Chicago Press, 2000), 567, §2, §5aα.

12. David E. Garland, *Luke*, Zondervan Exegetical Commentary on the New Testament (Grand Rapids: Zondervan, 2011), 636.

13. Garland, *Luke*, 624.

14. Kenneth E. Bailey, *Finding the Lost: Cultural Keys to Luke 15* (St. Louis: Concordia, 1992), 143–46.

15. Garland, *Luke*, 635.

16. Joel B. Green, *The Gospel of Luke*, New International Commentary on the New Testament (Grand Rapids: Eerdmans, 1997), 646.

17. Kenneth E. Bailey, *Through Peasant Eyes: More Lucan Parables, Their Culture and Style* (Grand Rapids: Eerdmans, 1980), 144–47.

18. Amy-Jill Levine and Ben Witherington III, *The Gospel of Luke*, New Cambridge Bible Commentary (Cambridge: Cambridge Univ. Press, 2018), 493.

Chapter 4: Tribalism

1. David P. Gushee, *After Evangelicalism: The Path to a New Christianity* (Louisville: Westminster John Knox, 2020), 36.
2. David W. Bebbington, *Evangelicalism in Modern Britain: A History from the 1730s to the 1980s* (London: Routledge, 1989), 2–17.
3. Thomas S. Kidd, *Who Is an Evangelical? The History of a Movement in Crisis* (New Haven, CT: Yale Univ. Press, 2019), 154.
4. Hans F. Bayer, "The Preaching of Peter in Acts," in *Witness to the Gospel: The Theology of Acts*, ed. I. Howard Marshall and David Peterson (Grand Rapids: Eerdmans, 1998), 257–74; G. Walter Hansen, "The Preaching and Defense of Paul," in Marshall and Peterson, *Witness to the Gospel*, 295–324.
5. For a recent attempt to show the integration of the four main atonement theories, see Joshua M. McNall, *The Mosaic of Atonement: An Integrated Approach to Christ's Work* (Grand Rapids: Zondervan Academic, 2019).
6. Dennis R. Edwards, *Might from the Margins: The Gospel's Power to Turn the Tables on Injustice* (Harrisonburg, VA: Herald Press, 2020), 28.
7. Edwards, *Might from the Margins*, 30.
8. Bebbington, *Evangelicalism in Modern Britain*, 12, 71–72.
9. Bebbington, *Evangelicalism in Modern Britain*, 188; David Goodhew, "The Rise of the Cambridge Inter-Collegiate Christian Union, 1910–1971," *Journal of Ecclesiastical History* 54, no. 1 (2003): 62–88.
10. Norman P. Grubb, *Once Caught, No Escape: My Life Story* (Cambridge: Lutterworth, 1969), 56; cited in John R. W. Stott, *The Cross of Christ* (Leicester: Inter-Varsity Press, 1986), 8.
11. Richard Quebedeaux, *The Young Evangelicals: Revolution in Orthodoxy* (New York: Harper and Row, 1974), 91–92.

12. Bebbington, *Evangelicalism in Modern Britain*, 188.
13. James D. Bratt, ed., *Abraham Kuyper: A Centennial Reader* (Grand Rapids: Eerdmans, 1998), 488.
14. Joseph H. Hellerman, *When the Church Was a Family: Recapturing Jesus' Vision for Authentic Christian Community* (Nashville: B&H Academic, 2009), 125.
15. Michael F. Bird, *Romans*, The Story of God Bible Commentary (Grand Rapids: Zondervan, 2016), 22.
16. Andrew D. Clarke, *Secular and Christian Leadership in Corinth: A Socio-Historical and Exegetical Study of 1 Corinthians 1–6*, Paternoster Biblical Monographs (Eugene, OR: Wipf and Stock, 2006), 92.
17. Roy E. Ciampa and Brian S. Rosner, *The First Letter to the Corinthians*, Pillar New Testament Commentary (Grand Rapids: Eerdmans, 2010), 81–82.
18. David E. Garland, *1 Corinthians*, Baker Exegetical Commentary on the New Testament (Grand Rapids: Baker Academic, 2003), 50–51.
19. Gordon D. Fee, *The First Epistle to the Corinthians*, New International Commentary on the New Testament, rev. ed. (Grand Rapids: Eerdmans, 2014), 60.
20. Doris Kearns Goodwin, *Team of Rivals: The Political Genius of Abraham Lincoln* (New York: Simon and Schuster, 2005).
21. Ross Douthat, *Bad Religion: How We Became a Nation of Heretics* (New York: Free Press, 2012), 11–12.

Chapter 5: Acceptable Sins

1. Natasha Percy, "Driscoll: Sydney You Have to Change!" Sydney Anglicans, September 3, 2008, https://sydneyanglicans.net/news/driscolls_back/.
2. Kate Shellnutt and Morgan Lee, "Mark Driscoll Resigns from Mars Hill," *Christianity Today*, October 15, 2014, www.christianitytoday.com/ct/2014/october-web-only/mark-driscoll-resigns-from-mars-hill.html.

3. Mike Cosper, *The Rise and Fall of Mars Hill* (podcast), June 2021–May 2022, www.christianitytoday.com/ct/podcasts/rise -and-fall-of-mars-hill/.

4. Joy Tibbs, "The Rise and Fall of Mark Driscoll," *Premier Christianity*, November 11, 2014, www.premierchristianity.com /home/the-rise-and-fall-of-mark-driscoll/761.article.

5. Julie Roys, "Hard Times at Harvest," *The Roys Report*, December 13, 2018, https://julieroys.com/hard-times-at-harvest/.

6. Kate Shellnutt, "Acts 29 CEO Removed amid 'Accusations of Abusive Leadership,'" *Christianity Today*, February 7, 2020, www.christianitytoday.com/news/2020/february/acts-29-ceo -steve-timmis-removed-spiritual-abuse-tch.html.

7. Scot McKnight and Laura Barringer, *A Church Called Tov: Forming a Goodness Culture That Resists Abuses of Power and Promotes Healing* (Carol Stream, IL: Tyndale Momentum, 2020), 5.

8. Timothy G. Gombis, *Mark*, The Story of God Bible Commentary (Grand Rapids: Zondervan Academic, 2021), 40.

9. Thomas R. Schreiner, *1 and 2 Peter and Jude*, Christian Standard Commentary (Nashville: Holman Reference, 2020), 277.

10. Douglas J. Moo, *The Letter of James: An Introduction and Commentary* (Leicester: Inter-Varsity Press, 1985), 150.

Chapter 6: Till Death Do Us Part

1. The submission of wives to their husbands is the most controversial element of marriage within evangelical circles. While wife submission remains the traditional, conservative, and dominant view, many evangelicals endorse the notion of mutual submission, based on Ephesians 5:21. This is a huge issue of its own but is not the concern in this chapter.

2. I say supposedly because the verse has traditionally been translated this way, but this was a mistake that has been corrected in more recent translations.

3. Gordon J. Wenham, "No Remarriage after Divorce," in *Remarriage after Divorce: Three Views in Today's Church*, Gordon J.

Wenham, William A. Heth, Craig S. Keener, ed. Mark L. Strauss (Grand Rapids: Zondervan, 2006), 19–42.

4. Victor P. Hamilton, *The Book of Genesis: Chapters 1–17*, New International Commentary on the Old Testament (Grand Rapids: Eerdmans, 1990), 175–76.

5. Frank Thielman, *Ephesians*, Baker Exegetical Commentary on the New Testament (Grand Rapids: Baker Academic, 2010), 389.

6. Michael H. Floyd, *Minor Prophets: Part 2*, The Forms of Old Testament Literature, vol. 22 (Grand Rapids: Eerdmans, 2000), 606–9.

7. Floyd, *Minor Prophets*, 609.

8. Roy E. Ciampa and Brian S. Rosner, *The First Letter to the Corinthians*, Pillar New Testament Commentary (Grand Rapids: Eerdmans, 2010), 302–3.

9. It is worth noting that the discussion in Matthew 19 occurs just as Jesus arrives in Perea, the domain of Herod Antipas, who had divorced his first wife, Phasaelis, to marry his niece, Herodias. This was all the more an issue since Herodias's husband, Philip, was still alive. She had divorced him to marry Antipas. The Pharisees were trying to make Jesus comment on Antipas's marriage, just down the road from where John the Baptist was executed for denouncing Antipas's marriage. I thank George Athas for pointing this out.

10. See Philo, *On the Special Laws* III:30, and Josephus, *Antiquities* 4:253; David E. Garland, *Reading Matthew: A Literary and Theological Commentary* (Macon: Smyth and Helwys, 2001), 202.

11. Garland, *Reading Matthew*, 202.

12. *Mishna Ketubot* 7:6; *Babylonian Talmud Gittin* 90b; Garland, *Reading Matthew*, 202.

13. R. T. France, *The Gospel according to Matthew: An Introduction and Commentary*, TNTC (Leicester: Inter-Varsity Press, 1985), 281.

14. Anthony C. Thiselton, *The First Epistle to the Corinthians: A Commentary on the Greek Text*, New International Greek Testament Commentary (Grand Rapids: Eerdmans, 2000), 537.

15. Some commentators understand the phrase "God has called us to live in peace" to refer to reconciliation rather than separation, based on the Hebrew meaning of peace—*shalom*—which indicates more than the cessation of hostilities but fullness and reconciliation (Gordon D. Fee, *The First Epistle to the Corinthians*, New International Commentary on the New Testament, rev. ed. [Grand Rapids: Eerdmans, 2014], 335–37). But as Thiselton cautions, "We should read neither too much nor too little from . . . in peace . . . it would be a mistake to read every nuance of the Hebrew word into Paul's contextually conditional use of the Greek here." Thiselton, *First Epistle to the Corinthians*, 637. Given its position in the flow of thought, it is more likely that the reference to living in peace means that believers are to find God's peace in every situation, even in divorce if necessary.

16. Rebecca Randall, "Wayne Grudem Changes Mind about Divorce in Cases of Abuse," *Christianity Today*, November 26, 2019, www.christianitytoday.com/news/2019/november /complementarian-wayne-grudem-ets-divorce-after-abuse.html.

17. George W. Knight, *The Pastoral Epistles: A Commentary on the Greek Text*, New International Greek Testament Commentary (Grand Rapids: Eerdmans, 1992), 157–59.

18. Wenham, "No Remarriage after Divorce."

19. Craig S. Keener, *Matthew*, IVP New Testament Commentary (Downers Grove, IL: InterVarsity, 1997), 298. For a fuller exposition of his views on remarriage after divorce, which are similar to those I've laid out, see Keener's chapter, "Remarriage for Circumstances beyond Adultery or Desertion," in Strauss, *Remarriage after Divorce in Today's Church*, 103–19.

20. David Instone-Brewer, *Divorce and Remarriage in the Church: Biblical Solutions for Pastoral Realities* (Milton Keynes: Paternoster, 2003), 84–85.

21. I'm so grateful for my extended family and friends who've done this for me and my wife, Niah. I'm also grateful for our Anglican church community, who've welcomed and accepted us.

Chapter 7: Megaperch Pastors

1. "Megachurch Definition," Hartford Institute for Religion Research, http://hirr.hartsem.edu/megachurch/definition.html. The Hartford Institute did not include Catholic megachurches in their study for a variety of reasons, mostly to do with their quite different structure and culture compared with typical Protestant megachurches.

2. Cathy Lynn Grossman, "The Megachurch Boom Rolls On, but Big Concerns Are Rising Too," *Religion News Service*, December 2, 2015, https://religionnews.com/2015/12/02/mega church-evangelical-christians/.

3. Warren Bird and Scott Thumma, "Megachurch 2020: The Changing Reality in America's Largest Churches," Hartford Institute for Religion Research, 2020, http://hirr.hartsem.edu /megachurch/2020_Megachurch_Report.pdf.

4. "Megachurch Definition," Hartford Institute for Religion Research.

5. "Megachurch Definition," Hartford Institute for Religion Research.

6. Mark Chaves, "All Creatures Great and Small: Megachurches in Context," *Religious Research* 47, no. 4 (2006): 337.

7. Scott Thumma and Warren Bird, "Not Who You Think They Are: A Profile of the People Who Attend America's Mega-churches," Hartford Institute for Religion Research, June 2009, http://hirr.hartsem.edu/megachurch/megachurch_attender _report.htm.

8. Chaves, "All Creatures Great and Small," 338.

9. This contradicts Thumma's 2007 work in which "These Churches Are Bad for Other Churches" is treated as a mega-church myth. But even the chapter on the subject more or less confirms that there is something to the myth. Thumma and Travis write, "Hard data to adequately address the question are limited. . . . So it is partly true that some people are drawn into large churches and that some megachurches aren't the best

playground partners." Scott Thumma and Dave Travis, *Beyond Megachurch Myths: What We Can Learn from America's Largest Churches* (San Francisco: Jossey-Bass, 2007), 124–25.

10. Bird and Thumma, "Megachurch 2020," 11.

11. "Prison, Jail, and Re-Entry," Willow Creek Care Center, www .willowcreekcarecenter.org/volunteer/prison-jail-and-re-entry/.

12. Bird and Thumma, "Megachurch 2020," 4.

13. Bird and Thumma, "Megachurch 2020," 12.

14. Mark J. Cartledge et al., *Megachurches and Social Engagement: Public Theology in Practice* (Leiden: Brill, 2019), 50.

15. Warren Cole Smith, "Guest Post: What Happened at Willow Creek?" *The Roys Report*, February 24, 2020, https://julieroys .com/guest-post-what-happened-at-willow-creek/.

16. Cole Smith, "Guest Post: What Happened at Willow Creek?"

17. Cole Smith, "Guest Post: What Happened at Willow Creek?"

18. Cole Smith, "Guest Post: What Happened at Willow Creek?"

19. Julie Roys, "Son of Former MBI President Joe Stowell Speaks of 'Toxic,' 'Unholy,' and 'Dangerous' Culture at Harvest," *The Roys Report*, December 22, 2018, https://julieroys.com/son-former -mbi-president-joe-stowell-speaks-toxic-unholy-dangerous -culture-harvest/.

20. Roys, "Son of Former MBI President."

21. Roys, "Son of Former MBI President."

22. Roys, "Son of Former MBI President."

23. Julie Roys, "Harvest Elder Dan George Offers Public Con- fession," *The Roys Report*, February 22, 2019, https://julieroys .com/harvest-elder-dan-george-offers-public-confession/.

24. Roys, "Harvest Elder Dan George."

25. Roys, "Harvest Elder Dan George."

26. Thumma and Travis, *Beyond Megachurch Myths*, 57–58.

27. Patricia Leigh Brown, "Megachurches as Minitowns," *New York Times*, May 9, 2002, www.nytimes.com/2002/05/09/garden /megachurches-as-minitowns.html.

28. Cartledge et al., *Megachurches and Social Engagement*, 52.

29. Jennifer Eaton Dyer, "The Core Beliefs of Southern Evangelicals: A Psycho-Social Investigation of the Evangelical Megachurch Phenomenon" (PhD diss., Vanderbilt University, 2007), 97.
30. Dyer, "Core Beliefs of Southern Evangelicals," 98.
31. Dyer, "Core Beliefs of Southern Evangelicals," 98.
32. Scot McKnight and Laura Barringer, *A Church Called Tov: Forming a Goodness Culture That Resists Abuses of Power and Promotes Healing* (Carol Stream, IL: Tyndale Momentum, 2020), 18.
33. Brown, "Megachurches as Minitowns."
34. Brown, "Megachurches as Minitowns."
35. Brown, "Megachurches as Minitowns."
36. Dyer, "Core Beliefs of Southern Evangelicals," 106.
37. Dyer, "Core Beliefs of Southern Evangelicals," 84.
38. Paul Lundquist, "Guest Post: Open Letter to Julie Roys," *The Roys Report*, January 5, 2020, https://julieroys.com/guest-post-open-letter-to-julie-roys/.
39. Geoff Surratt, Greg Ligon, and Warren Bird, *The Multi-site Church Revolution: Being One Church in Many Locations* (Grand Rapids: Zondervan, 2006), 18.
40. David W. Jones, "The Virtual Pastor: How Video Preaching Affects Those Who View It" (DMin diss., Phoenix Seminary, 2018), 3.
41. Jones, "Virtual Pastor," 4.
42. Jones, "Virtual Pastor," 5.
43. Jones, "Virtual Pastor," 5.
44. Jones, "Virtual Pastor," 5–6.
45. Jones, "Virtual Pastor," 137.
46. Jones, "Virtual Pastor," 138.
47. Jones, "Virtual Pastor," 138.
48. Jones, "Virtual Pastor," 145.
49. Jones, "Virtual Pastor," 146.
50. Jones, "Virtual Pastor," 149.
51. Jones, "Virtual Pastor," 168.
52. Jones, "Virtual Pastor," 168–69.

53. Thabiti Anyabwile, "Multi-site Churches Are from the Devil," Gospel Coalition, September 27, 2011, www.thegospelcoalition .org/blogs/thabiti-anyabwile/multi-site-churches-are-from-the -devil/.

54. "About," 9Marks, www.9marks.org/about/.

55. "Multi-site Churches," special issue, *9Marks Journal*, May–June 2009, www.9marks.org/journal/multi-site-churches/.

56. Jonathan Leeman, "The Alternative: Why Don't We Plant?" *9Marks Journal*, February 26, 2010, www.9marks.org/article /alternative-why-dont-we-plant/.

57. Leeman, "The Alternative."

58. Brad House and Gregg Allison, *Multichurch: Exploring the Future of Multisite* (Grand Rapids: Zondervan, 2017), 16, emphasis in original. Their concerns and criticisms of video -preaching multisite churches are found on pages 77–95.

59. House and Allison, *Multichurch*, 17.

60. House and Allison, *Multichurch*, 17.

61. Scott Thumma, "Exploring the Megachurch Phenomena: Their Characteristics and Cultural Context," Hartford Institute for Religion Research, 1996, http://hirr.hartsem.edu/bookshelf /thumma_article2.html.

62. "Megachurch Definition," Hartford Institute for Religion Research, http://hirr.hartsem.edu/megachurch/definition.html.

63. Bird and Thumma, "Megachurch 2020," 13.

64. Thumma, "Exploring the Megachurch Phenomena."

65. Scott Christian, "WWJD: The Ethical Conundrum of Mega-church Preachers in Super-Expensive Sneakers," *Esquire*, April 12, 2019, www.esquire.com/style/mens-fashion/a27114633 /expensive-sneakers-preachers-sneakersnpreachers-instagram -interview/.

66. Hannah Frishberg, "Tithe Money Funded Hillsong Pastors' Luxury Lifestyles: Former Members," *New York Post*, January 26, 2021, https://nypost.com/2021/01/26/former-hillsong-members -detail-pastors-lavish-lifestyles/.

67. Warren Cole Smith, "Unreal Sales for Driscoll's *Real Marriage*," *World*, March 5, 2014, https://wng.org/sift/unreal-sales-for-driscolls-real-marriage-1617422429.

68. Jeremy Burns, "Mark Driscoll Admits 'Manipulating' Book Best-Seller System," *Christian Retailing*, May 14, 2014, www.christianretailing.com/index.php/news/industry-news/27025-mark-driscoll-admits-manipulating-book-best-seller-system.

69. Jeff Bercovici, "Firm That Helps Authors Buy Their Way onto Bestseller Lists Goes into Stealth Mode," *Forbes*, April 18, 2014, www.forbes.com/sites/jeffbercovici/2014/04/18/firm-that-helps-authors-buy-their-way-onto-bestseller-lists-goes-into-stealth-mode/?sh=2eca7e345f52.

70. Andreas J. Köstenberger, *John*, Baker Exegetical Commentary on the New Testament (Grand Rapids: Baker Academic, 2004), 304–6.

71. Harold W. Hoehner, *Ephesians: An Exegetical Commentary* (Grand Rapids: Baker Academic, 2002), 543–45.

72. David F. Wells, *Above All Earthly Pow'rs: Christ in a Postmodern World* (Grand Rapids: Eerdmans, 2005), 119.

73. Lundquist, "Guest Post: Open Letter to Julie Roys," emphasis in original.

Chapter 8: The Lunatic Fringe

1. David W. Bebbington, *Evangelicalism in Modern Britain: A History from the 1730s to the 1980s* (London: Routledge, 1989), 2–17.

2. Fred Clark, "The 'Weird Fringe' Is the Biggest Part of White Evangelicalism," in *Evangelicals: Who They Have Been, Are Now, and Could Be*, ed. Mark A. Noll, David W. Bebbington, and George M. Marsden (Grand Rapids: Eerdmans, 2019), Kindle loc. 5194–259.

3. Adam Brewster and Caitlin Huey-Burns, "Former Republican Officials Consider Splitting from GOP to Form New Party," *CBS News*, February 12, 2021, www.cbsnews.com/news/new-republican-party-former-gop-officials-trump/.

4. Clark, "'Weird Fringe,'" Kindle loc. 5194.

5. Michael Brice-Saddler, "A Wealthy Televangelist Explains His Fleet of Private Jets: 'It's a Biblical Thing,'" *Washington Post*, June 3, 2019, www.washingtonpost.com/religion/2019/06/04/wealthy-televangelist-explains-his-fleet-private-jets-its-biblical-thing/.

6. Alex Woodward, "Coronavirus: Televangelist Kenneth Copeland 'Blows Wind of God' at Covid-19 to 'Destroy' Pandemic," *Independent*, April 6, 2020, www.independent.co.uk/news/world/americas/kenneth-copeland-blow-coronavirus-pray-sermon-trump-televangelist-a9448561.html.

7. Conor Gaffey, "Who Is Paula White, Donald Trump's Favorite Pastor?" *Newsweek*, August 25, 2017, www.newsweek.com/president-donald-trump-paula-white-prosperity-gospel-655064.

8. Norman C. Habel, *The Book of Job: A Commentary* (London: SCM, 1985), 80–91.

9. William Steuart McBirnie, *The Search for the Twelve Apostles* (Carol Stream, IL: Tyndale Momentum, 1973).

10. Ross Douthat, *Bad Religion: How We Became a Nation of Heretics* (New York: Free Press, 2012), 207.

11. Andreas J. Köstenberger, *Commentary on 1–2 Timothy and Titus*, Biblical Theology for Christian Proclamation (Nashville: Holman Reference, 2017), 264.

12. Douthat, *Bad Religion*, 182.

13. Sheanne Aguila, "Joel Osteen Net Worth 2017: About the Fifty-Four-Year-Old Evangelist, Lakewood Church and His River Oaks Home," *Christian Post*, August 31, 2017, www.christianpost.com/news/joel-osteen-net-worth-2017-how-rich-is-the-54-year-old-evangelist-197347/.

14. Edward Luce, "A Preacher for Trump's America: Joel Osteen and the Prosperity Gospel," *Financial Times*, April 18, 2019, www.ft.com/content/3990ce66-60a6-11e9-b285-3acd5d43599e.

15. Joe Carter, "What Kanye Should Know about Joel Osteen,"

Gospel Coalition, November 15, 2019, www.thegospelcoalition
.org/article/what-kanye-should-know-about-joel-osteen/.

16. Luce, "Preacher for Trump's America."

17. Luce, "Preacher for Trump's America."

18. Luce, "Preacher for Trump's America."

19. Douthat, *Bad Religion*, 183.

20. Jeremy W. Peters and Elizabeth Dias, "Paula White, Newest White House Aide, Is a Uniquely Trumpian Pastor," *New York Times*, November 2, 2019, www.nytimes.com/2019/11/02/us /politics/paula-white-trump.html.

21. Peters and Dias, "Paula White, Newest White House Aide."

22. Rachel Zoll, "Televangelists Escape Penalty in Senate Inquiry," *NBC News*, January 7, 2011, www.nbcnews.com/id /wbna40960871.

23. Jason Lemon, "Trump Spiritual Adviser Paula White Prays against President's Opponents, Suggests They 'Operate in Sorcery and Witchcraft,'" *Newsweek*, November 6, 2019, www .newsweek.com/trump-spiritual-adviser-paula-white-prays -against-presidents-opponents-suggests-they-operate-1470197.

24. Lemon, "Trump Spiritual Adviser Paula White."

25. Lemon, "Trump Spiritual Adviser Paula White."

26. Wyatte Grantham-Philips, "Pastor Paula White Calls on Angels from Africa and South America to Bring Trump Victory," *USA Today*, November 6, 2020, www.usatoday.com/story/news/nation /2020/11/05/paula-white-trumps-spiritual-adviser-african-south -american-angels/6173576002/.

27. Grantham-Philips, "Pastor Paula White Calls on Angels."

28. Michael Gryboski, "John MacArthur Says 'True Believers' Will Vote for Trump, Can't Affirm Abortion and Trans Activism," *Christian Post*, September 2, 2020, www.christianpost.com/news /john-macarthur-says-true-believers-will-vote-for-trump-cant -affirm-abortion-and-trans-activism.html.

29. *God Bless the USA Bible*, https://godblesstheusabible.com.

30. Robert N. Bellah, "Civil Religion in America," *Daedalus* 96, no. 1 (1967): 1–21.
31. Bellah, "Civil Religion in America," 8.
32. Bellah, "Civil Religion in America," 8.
33. Bellah, "Civil Religion in America," 13.
34. Bellah, "Civil Religion in America," 18.
35. David Brooks, "Who Is John Stott?" *New York Times*, November 30, 2004, www.nytimes.com/2004/11/30/opinion/who-is-john-stott.html.
36. Billy Graham, "John Stott," The 2005 Time 100, *Time*, April 18, 2005, http://content.time.com/time/specials/packages/article/0,28804,1972656_1972717_1974108,00.html.
37. "John Stott Dies at Ninety," Langham Partnership, July 27, 2011, https://uk.langham.org/john-stott-dies-at-90/.

Chapter 9: Saving Faith

1. Dallas Willard and Gary Black Jr., *The Divine Conspiracy Continued: Fulfilling God's Kingdom on Earth* (New York: HarperOne, 2014), 79.
2. Mark R. Glanville and Luke Glanville, *Refuge Reimagined: Biblical Kinship in Global Politics* (Downers Grove, IL: IVP Academic, 2021), 33.
3. Thomas Howard, *Evangelical Is Not Enough* (Nashville: Thomas Nelson, 1984), 1.
4. Russell Moore, "Why This Election Makes Me Hate the Word 'Evangelical,'" *Washington Post*, February 29, 2016, www.washingtonpost.com/news/acts-of-faith/wp/2016/02/29/russell-moore-why-this-election-makes-me-hate-the-word-evangelical/.
5. Thomas S. Kidd, "Is the Term 'Evangelical' Redeemable?" in *Evangelicals: Who They Have Been, Are Now, and Could Be*, ed. Mark A. Noll, David W. Bebbington, and George M. Marsden (Grand Rapids: Eerdmans, 2019), Kindle loc. 5270, emphasis in original.
6. Timothy Keller, "Can Evangelicalism Survive Donald Trump?"

in *Evangelicals: Who They Have Been, Are Now, and Could Be*, ed. Mark A. Noll, David W. Bebbington, and George M. Marsden (Grand Rapids: Eerdmans, 2019), Kindle loc. 5374.

7. *Oxford English Dictionary*, s.v. "literally," www.oed.com/view dictionaryentry/Entry/109061, accessed June 2022.

8. Mark Noll, *The Scandal of the Evangelical Mind* (Grand Rapids: Eerdmans, 1994), 115.

9. Moore, "Why This Election Makes Me Hate the Word 'Evangelical.'"

10. According to historian Mark Noll, "Fundamentalism created major problems in several ways for the life of the mind. First, it gave a new impetus to general anti-intellectualism; second, it hardened conservative evangelical commitments to certain features of nineteenth-century evangelical-American synthesis that were problematic to begin with; and third, its major theological emphases had a chilling effect on the exercise of Christian thinking about the world." Noll, *Scandal of the Evangelical Mind*, 115. For a broader discussion of the issues, see pp. 114–45.

11. Kristin Kobes Du Mez, *Jesus and John Wayne: How White Evangelicals Corrupted a Faith and Fractured a Nation* (New York: Liveright, 2020), 21.

12. Kidd, "Is the Term 'Evangelical' Redeemable?" Kindle loc. 5301.

13. In David Gushee's book *After Evangelicalism*, an appendix, "Toward a Post-evangelical Typology," is contributed by Isaiah Ritzmann, who groups post-evangelicals in three categories: "Still-Vangelicals" (who are more or less evangelical in conviction but do not identify with evangelical culture and politics), "Still Christians" (who are no longer evangelical in theology or culture but remain believing Christians of one sort or another), and "Still People" (who have left Christianity behind entirely). David P. Gushee, *After Evangelicalism: The Path to a New Christianity* (Louisville: Westminster John Knox, 2020), 171–73.

14. Apart from being a more elegant term, *exangelical* matches the ancient Greek word *exangello*, which means "to call out" (just

as *evangelical* derives from the Greek *evangel*, the good news). With such a term, exangelicals could identify themselves as those who wish to call out the problems and deficiencies within evangelicalism.